Drama Surrounded by Splendor

Men and Women at Work in Jean-François Millet's Paintings

By Mariella Carlotti

Art Direction By Andrea Benzoni

Photo
Archivio Scala Firenze,
Museum of Fine Arts, Boston
Museo Stedelijk Amsterdam
Bridgeman Art Library
Getty Images

Powered by
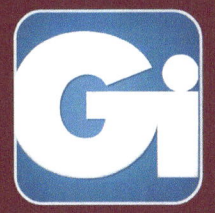
www.concreo.eu

Sponsor
Gi Group
YOUR JOB, OUR WORK

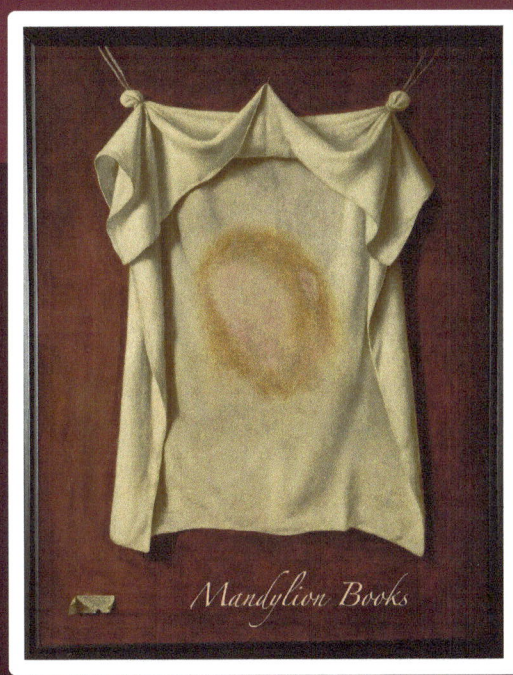

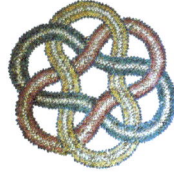

An imprint of **Revolution of Tenderness**
Copyright © 2017 Suzanne Lewis
All rights reserved.
ISBN-13: 978-1975813796
ISBN-10: 1975813790

BETWEEN NORMANDY AND PARIS 1814 -1849

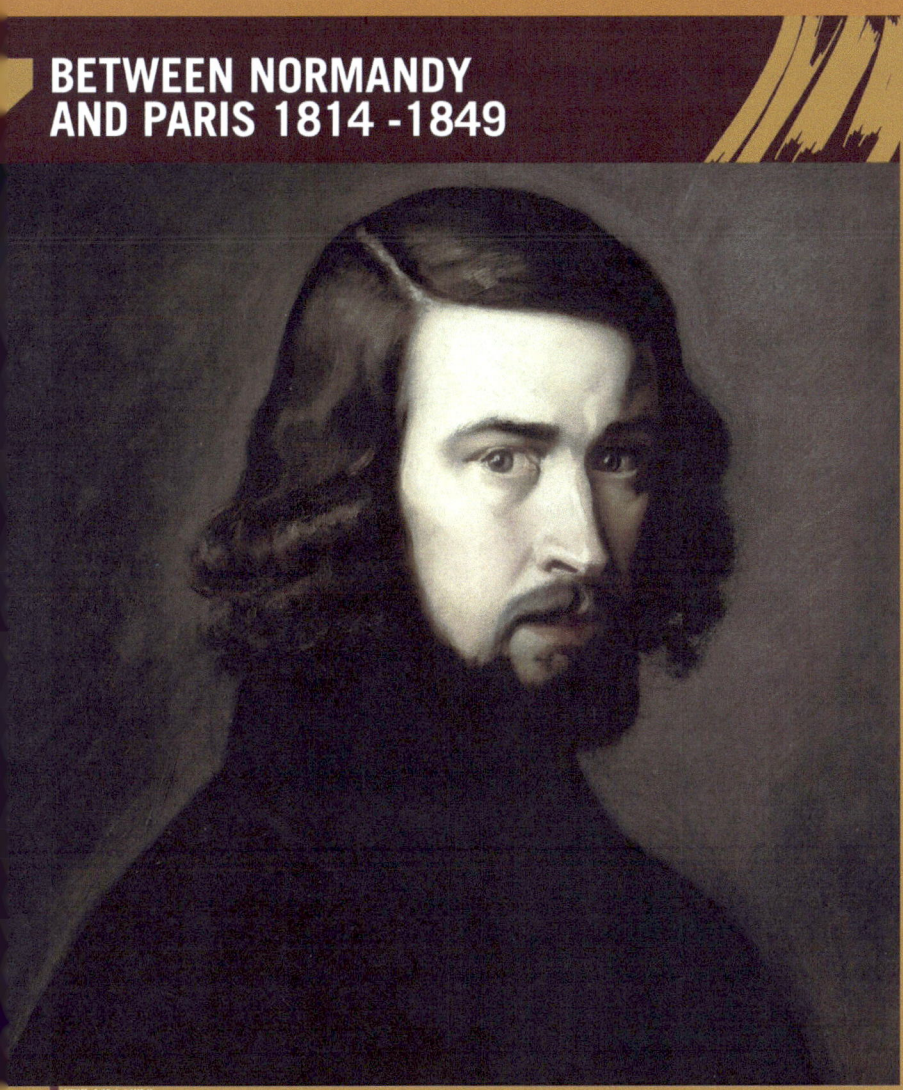

The general disaffectedness with labor, wrote **Charles Péguy** in 1910, *is the most profound defect, the fundamental defect of the modern world.* *
Some decades earlier, a French artist, **Jean-François Millet**, had chosen work – labor – as the preferred subject matter for his paintings: his works are charged with a sincere depth of feeling for the daily toil of humankind. Labor, as depicted by Millet, has an epic quality which, while safeguarding the dignity of the individual, highlights the contribution of work, in its transfiguration of the land, to the common good.

* *Unofficial translation from Notre Jeunesse [Our Youth], by Charles Péguy, Cahiers de la Quinzaine (Paris), 1910.*

Jean François Millet was born on October 4, 1814, into a family of peasant farmers in **Gruchy**, in the commune of Gréville (Normandy). As his date of birth coincided with the feast day of Saint Francis of Assisi, one of his given names was decided by simple tradition. **Alfred Sensier**, friend and biographer of Millet, perceptively remarked: *Saint Francis of Assisi, that faithful observer of the things of nature, was a happy choice of saint for the man who, later, was to be a passionate lover of the works of God* Jean-François was the first of nine children in a large and extended family that also included his grandmother, a great aunt, and a great uncle, Charles Millet, who was a priest. The Millets were small landowners, possessing property sufficient to ensure that the family could live comfortably. With a priest in the family, the cultural education of the young François was sure to be thorough and solid. Under Charles Millet, the boy learned to read, acquired Latin and possibly Greek, and grew to love great literature, influenced by the Bible and Virgil, especially his poem in four books, the **Georgics**.

Having exhibited a talent for drawing at an early age, in **1835** he moved to **Cherbourg** and began working with local artists, although it would be on visits to the city's recently opened Musée des Beaux Arts that he fashioned his artistic apprenticeship. Here, he was able to see at first hand Nicolas Poussin's Pietà, a work that Millet would always consider to be his model, his guiding light. While in Cherbourg, he restricted himself to drawing, and only began painting in 1837 when, having moved to Paris, he attended the École des Beaux Arts and became a pupil of **Paul Delaroche**. *Paris appeared to me dismal and insipid. I spent my first night in one continual nightmare. I saw again my native village ... my grandmother, mother, and sister sitting there spinning silk, weeping, and thinking of me, praying that I might escape from the perdition of Paris. I saw no one, did not speak to a soul, and hardly dared ask a question of anyone, so great was my fear of ridicule.** During these years, up until 1849, he lived alternately between Cherbourg and Paris and dedicated his efforts in particular to portraiture, for obvious reasons of income, given the demand for such work from the bourgeoisie of the time.

In 1842, he married **Pauline-Virginie Ono**, who died just two years later of consumption. Immediately after the death of his first wife, Millet met **Catherine Lemaire**, a young maid — much younger than he was — who would become his lifelong companion and bear him nine children. They married under civil law in 1853 — after the birth of their fourth child — only solemnizing the union in church much later, shortly before the painter's death. It was at this time that he met artists like **Théodore Rousseau**, **Charles Émile Jacque**, **Honoré Daumier**, **Antoine-Louis Barye**, and **Alfred Sensier**, who would become his friend and biographer.

**This and all following Millet quotes (except where otherwise referenced) have been unofficially translated from La Vie et L'Oeuvre de J.-F. Millet (The Life and Work of J.-F. Millet), by Alfred Sensier, A. Quantin (Paris), 1881.*

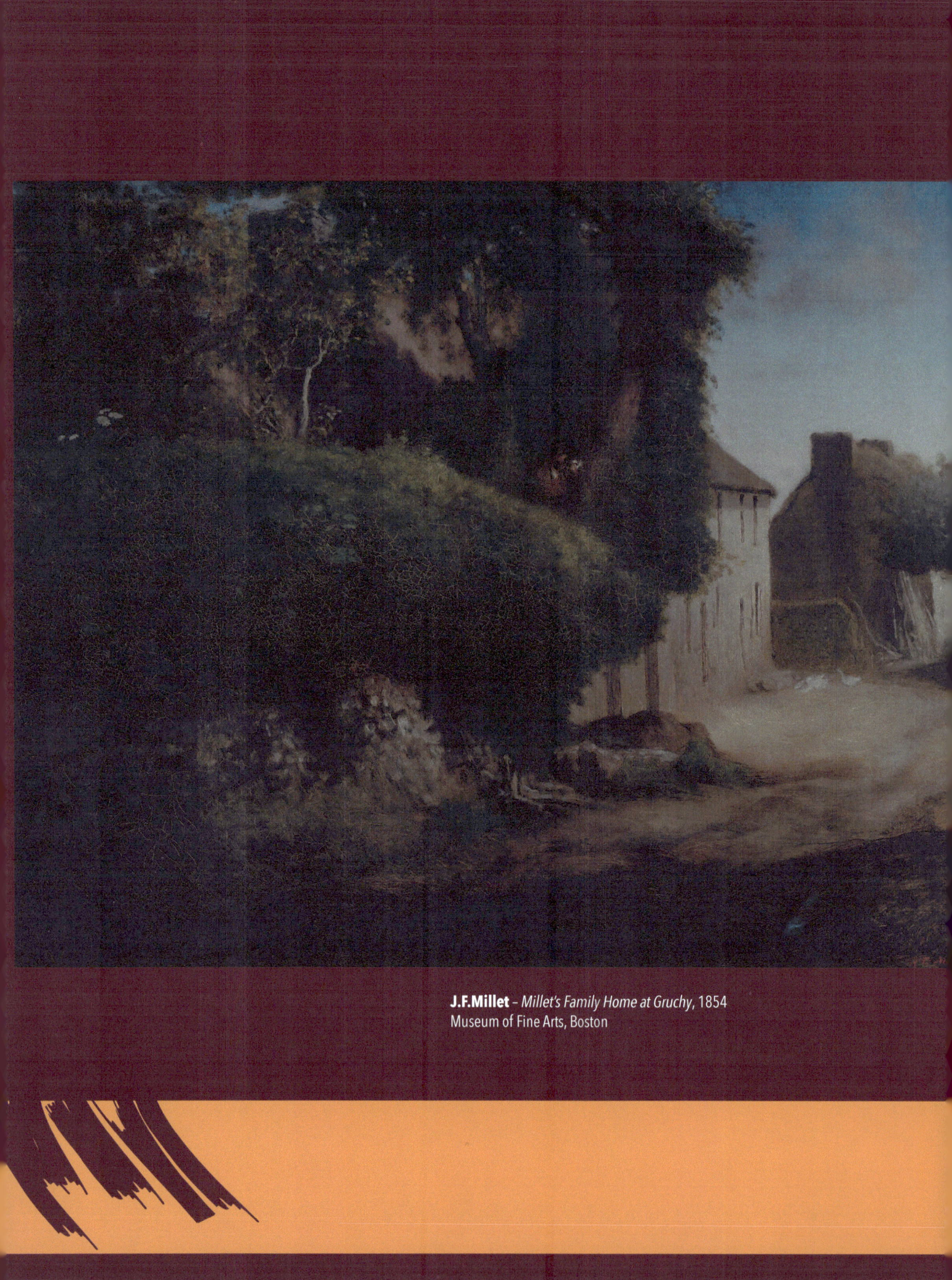

J.F.Millet – *Millet's Family Home at Gruchy*, 1854
Museum of Fine Arts, Boston

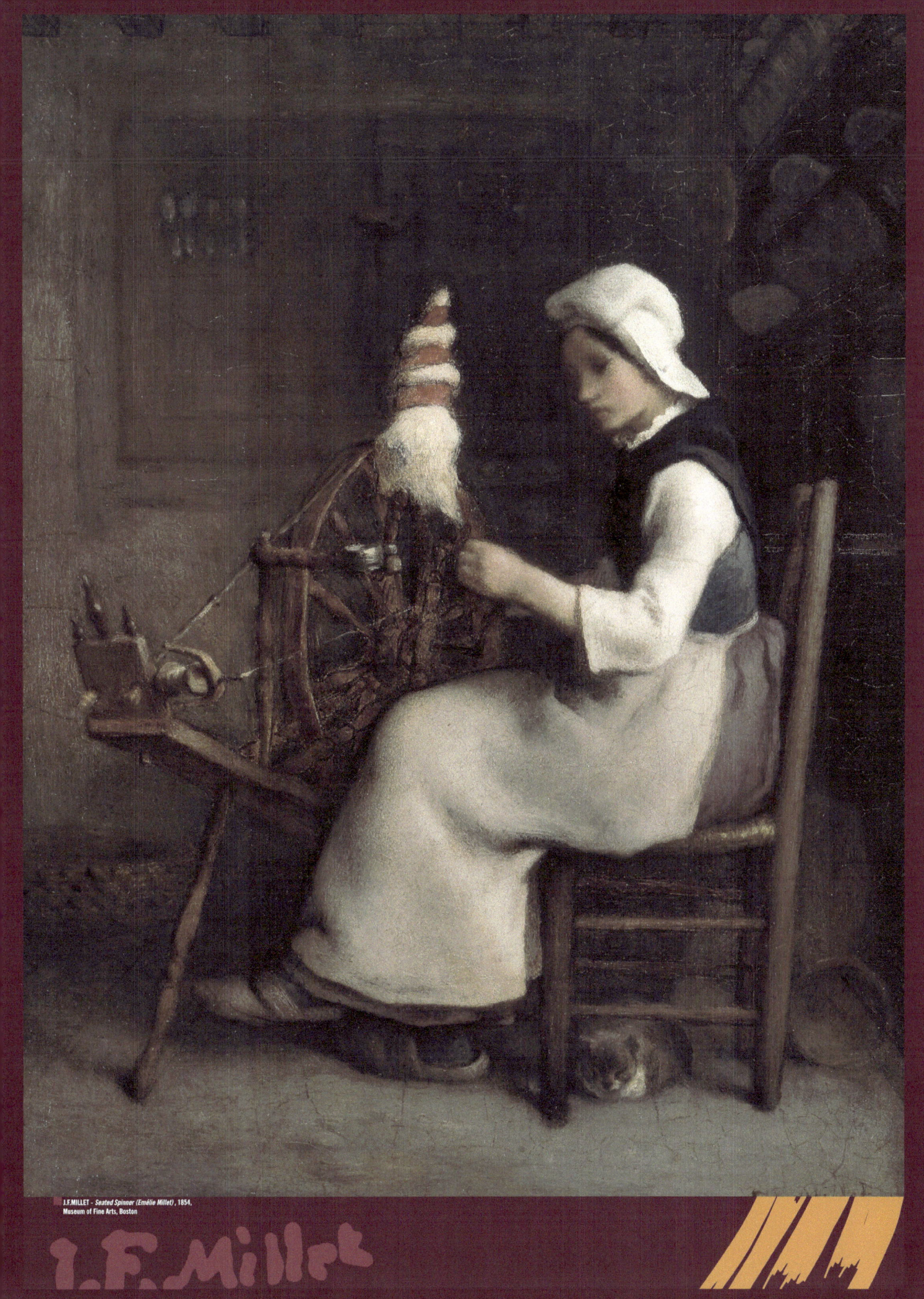

J.F. MILLET - *Seated Spinner (Emélie Millet)*, 1854, Museum of Fine Arts, Boston

BARBIZON 1849 - 1875

This depicts a scene from the Old Testament, already painted by the great French artist Poussin, whom Millet regarded as a master: the rich man **Boaz** approaches his reapers, who are busy eating, and introduces **Ruth**, the poor gleaner who would ultimately become his wife. This is a Bible story of the distant past told with simplicity using the language of the present. Millet considered this, his most complex work, the most important he had ever painted.

J.F.MILLET - *Harvesters Resting (Ruth and Boaz)*,
1850-1853, Museum of Fine Arts, Boston

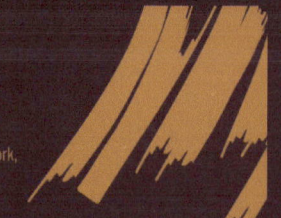

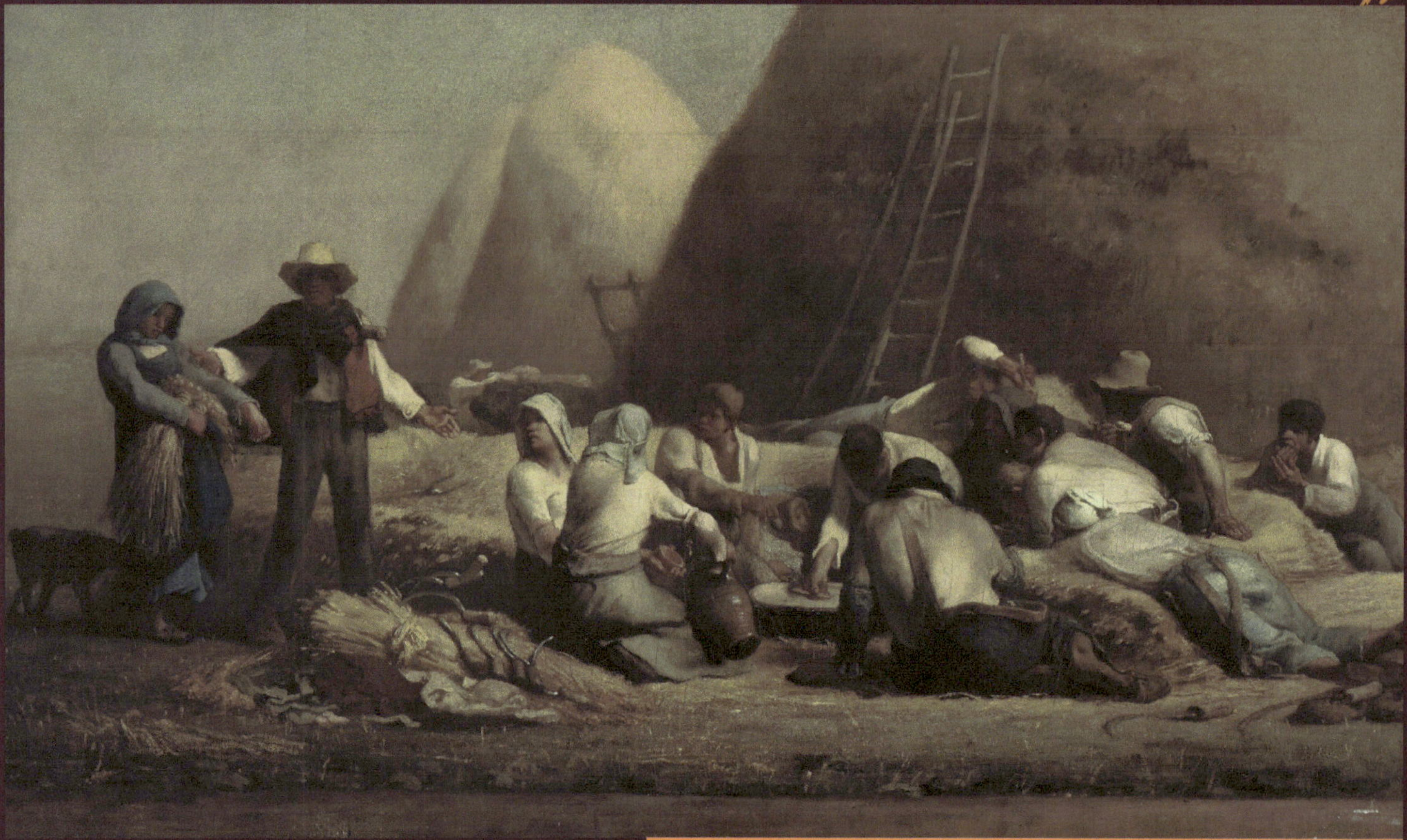

> I have to say that what moves my art is the human condition, the value of humanity.

In 1849, there was a major outbreak of cholera in Paris. Millet moved to Barbizon, where other painters already lived - Corot, Rousseau, and Daubigny, to name a few - having chosen this village, not far from the city, as an ideal location for serious artists to live and work. The history of art refers to this group of painters as the ***Barbizon School***. It was landscape painting that provided the focus for most of the group, given the proximity of the Forêt de Fontainebleau, but Millet was drawn more to life in the fields, and to the daily toil of peasant farmers. The stay at Barbizon - which Millet imagined initially to be temporary - became permanent, as he now found his vocation as a realist painter of these country people at their labor.

Ten years later, wearing the mask of a critic, Millet would confirm the judgement of his work given by others:

"Millet, more precisely, is rustic, in the true sense of the word... he is struck especially by the man who from birth is destined to live by toiling on the land, in the sense of that terrible verse of the Scriptures: "Thou shalt eat bread in the sweat of thy brow." And the reason is not hard to understand, given that he was brought up seeing only such things as these, and being a part of them". *

*Unofficial translation from Millet: Sessanta capolavori dal Museum of Fine Arts di Boston
[Millet: Sixty Masterpieces from the Museum of Fine Arts of Boston],
edited by Marco Goldin and George T.M. Shackelford, Linea D'Ombra Libri (Conegliano, Italy), 2004.

J.F.MILLET - *Harvesters Resting (Ruth and Boaz) details*
1850-1853, Museum of Fine Arts, Boston

J.F. Millet

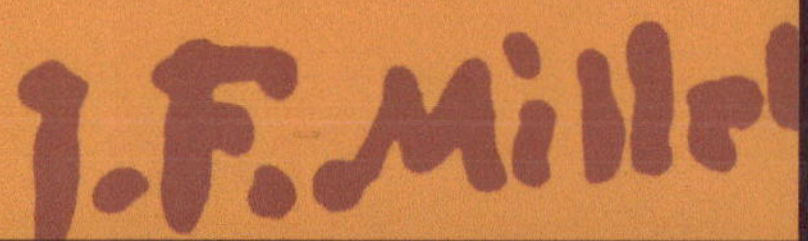

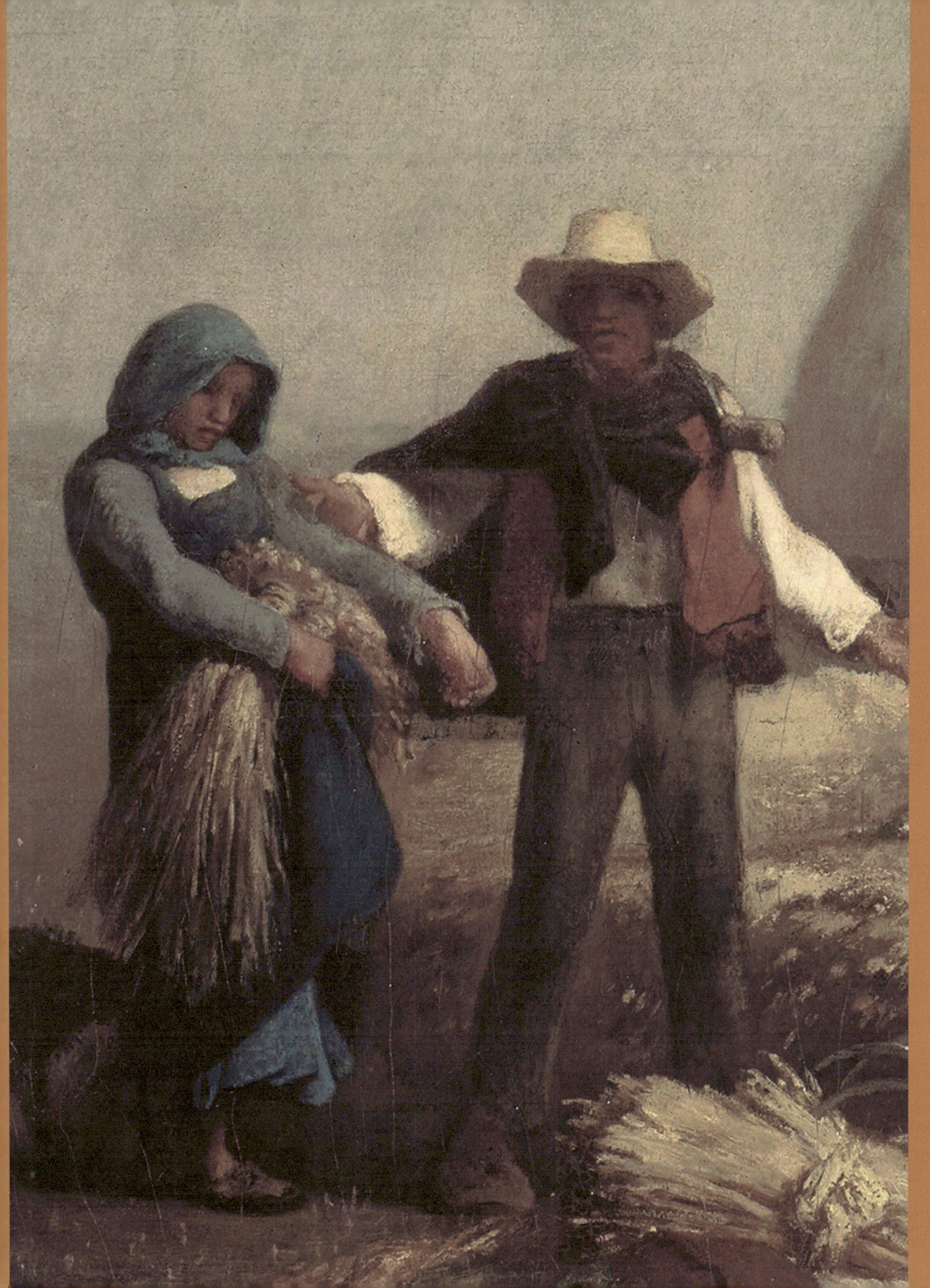

THE HUMAN ASPECT OF LABOR

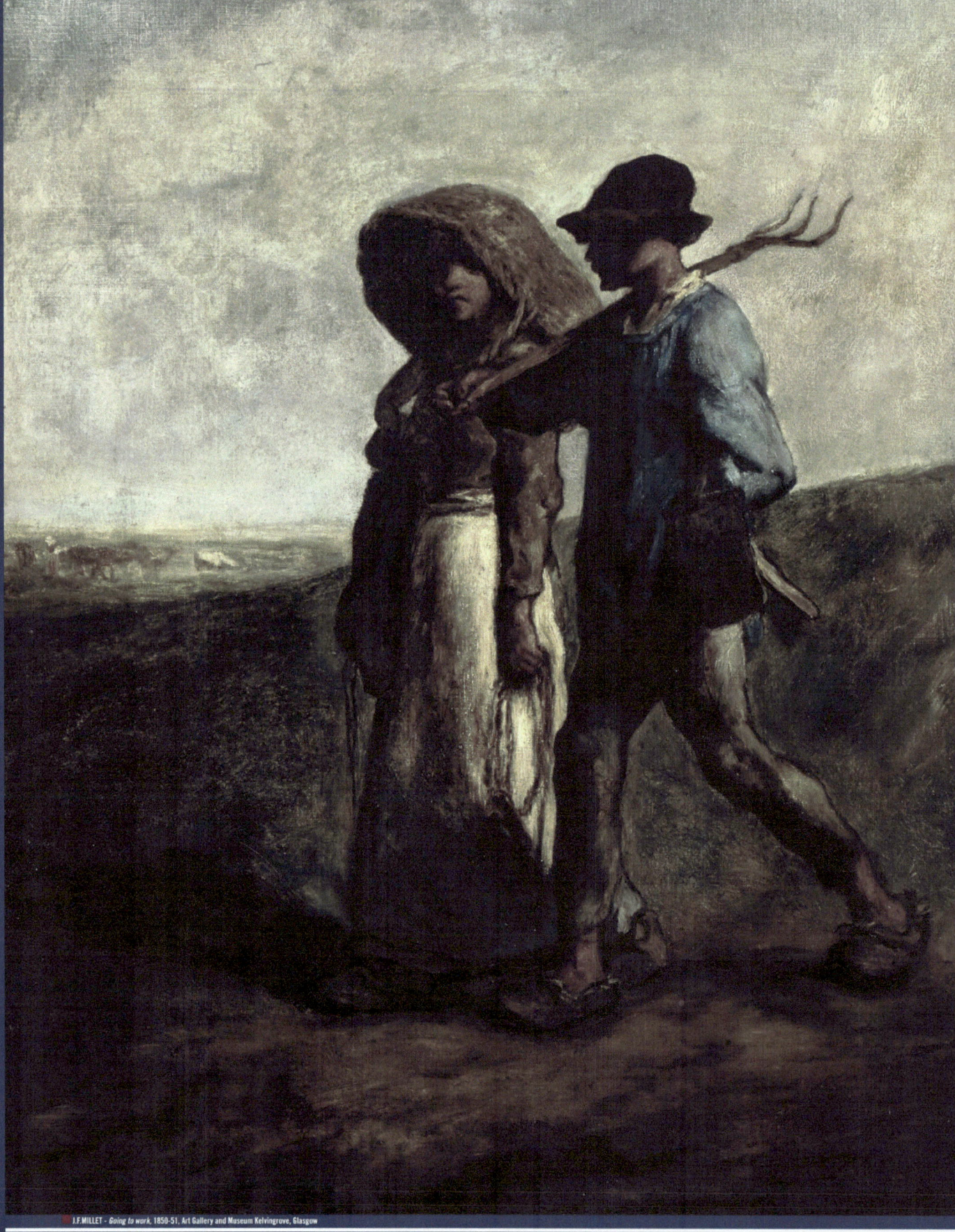

J.F. MILLET - *Going to work*, 1850-51, Art Gallery and Museum Kelvingrove, Glasgow

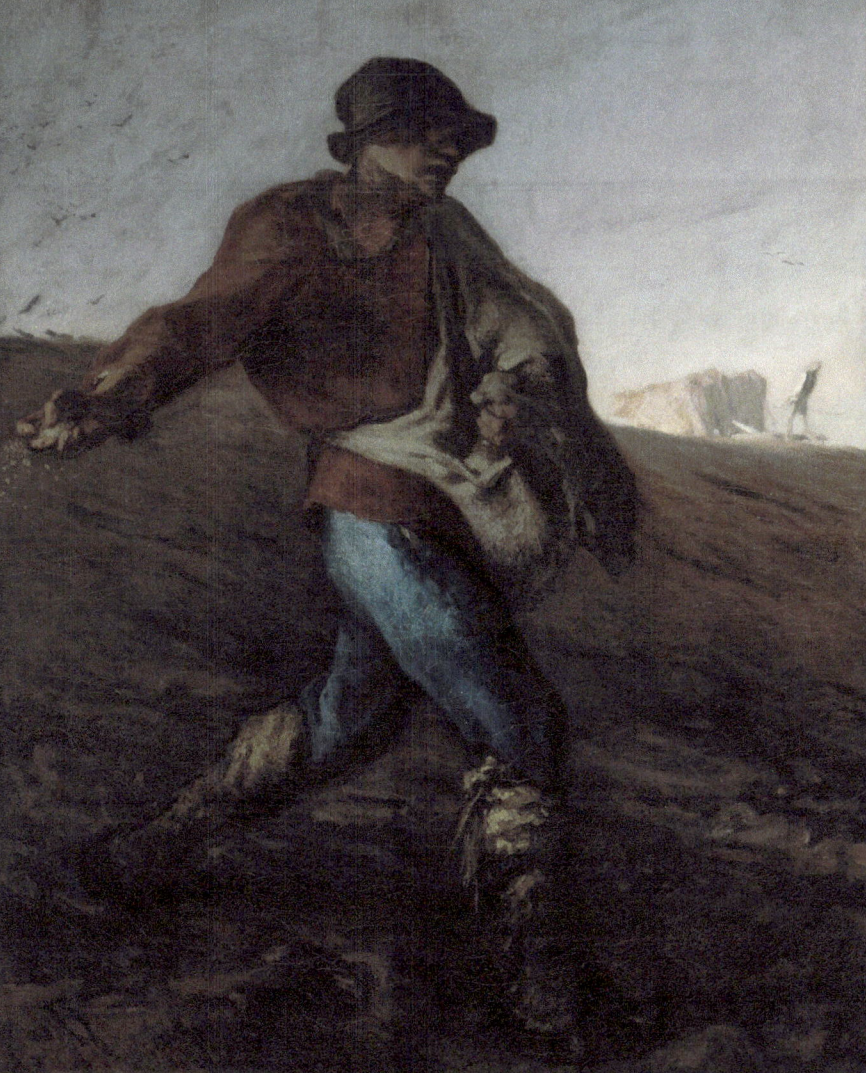

J.F. MILLET - The Sower 1850, Museum of Fine Arts, Boston

The Sower is Millet's first major masterpiece, which achieved significant public acclaim. With this painting, a year after moving to Barbizon, the artist embarked on a new and definitive phase in his career.

My program is work. That is the natural condition of humanity.

"In the sweat of thy brow thou shalt eat bread" was written centuries ago. The destiny of man is immutable, and can never change. What each one of us has to do is to seek progress in his profession, to try and improve daily in his trade ... and in this way to surpass his neighbor, both in the superiority of his talent and in the conscientiousness of his work. That is the only path for me.
All else is a dream or a lottery.

J.F. Millet

As you will see by the titles of the pictures, there are neither nude women nor mythological subjects among them. I mean to devote myself to other subjects; not that I hold that sort of thing to be forbidden, but that I do not wish to feel myself compelled to paint them ... peasant-subjects suit my nature best, for I must confess, at the risk of your taking me to be a Socialist, that the human side is what touches me most in art, and that if I could only do what I like, or at least attempt to do it, I would paint nothing that was not the result of an impression directly received from Nature, whether in landscape or in figures. The joyous side never shows itself to me; I know not if it exists, but I have never seen it. The gayest thing I know is the calm, the silence, which are so delicious, both in the forest and in the cultivated fields. You will confess that it always gives you a very dreamy sensation, and that the dream is a sad one, although often very delicious. ...In cultivated land sometimes as in places where the ground is barren you see figures digging and hoeing. From time to time, one raises himself and straightens his back, wiping his forehead with the back of his hand. "Thou shalt eat bread in the sweat of thy brow." Is this the gay and playful kind of work that some people would have us believe? Nevertheless, for me it is true humanity and great poetry.
(A Letter to Alfred Sensier, 1815, february 1th)

The first section contains pictures highlighting the daily toil of those who work the land, a back-breaking occupation that Millet saw as noble and heroic. It is not labor as sociologically defined or politically interpreted that interests Millet. The focus of his painting is people - people at work. Writing to his friend Sensier, he says, *I have to say that what moves my art is the human condition, the value of humanity.*

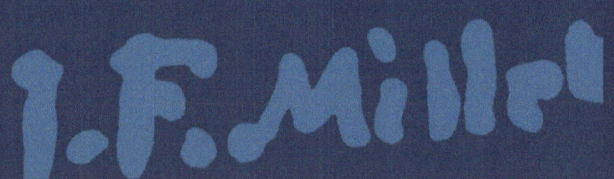

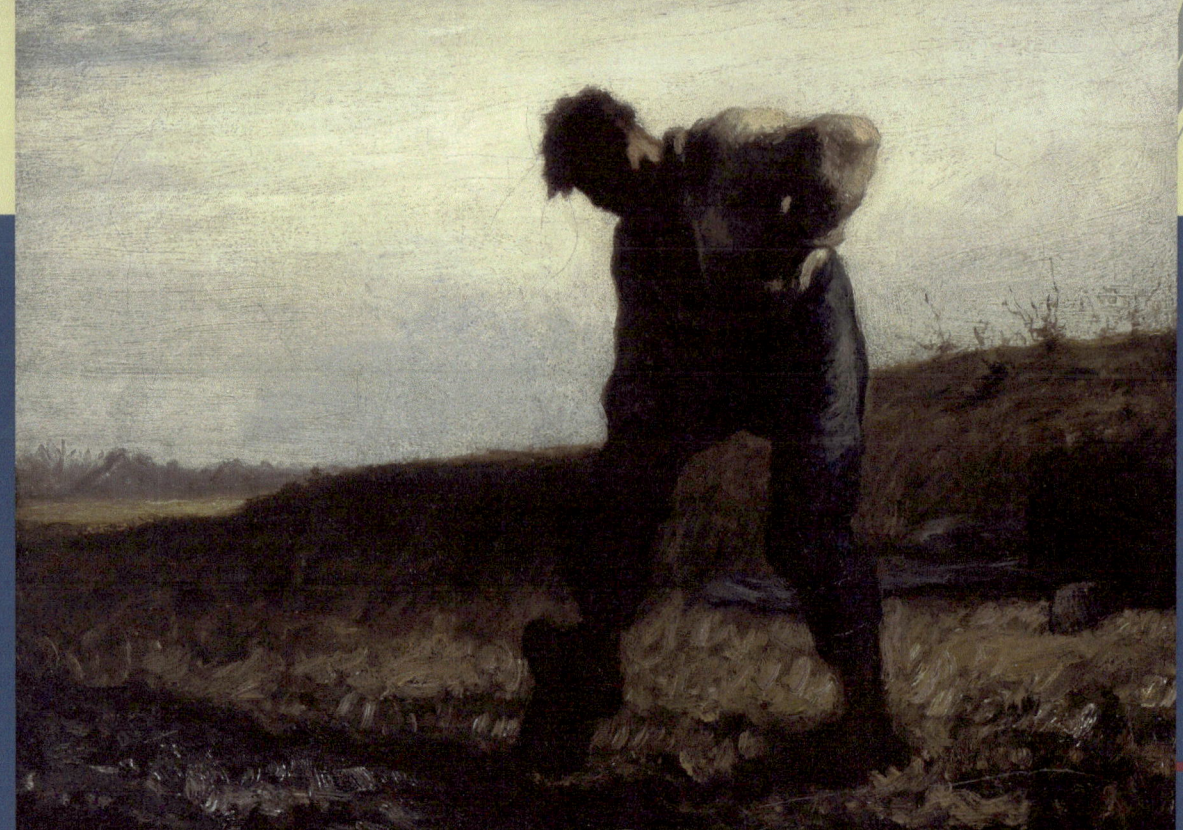

J.F. MILLET - Man Turning over the Soil, 1847-1850, Museum of Fine Arts, Boston

Every subject is good. All we have to do is to render it with force and clearness. In art, we should have one leading thought, and see that we express it in eloquent language, that we keep it alive in ourselves, and impart it to others as clearly as we stamp a medal. Art is not a pleasure trip. It is a battle, a mill that grinds. I am no philosopher. I do not pretend to do away with pain, or to find a formula which will make me a Stoic, and indifferent to evil. Suffering is, perhaps, the one thing that gives an artist power to express himself clearly.

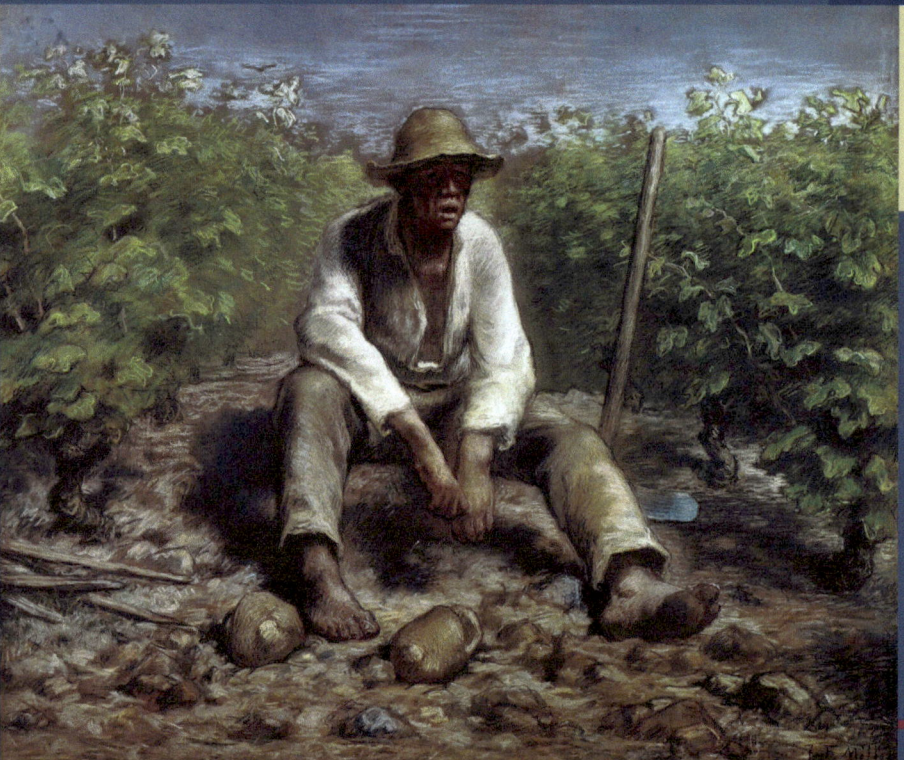

J.F. MILLET - The Vinedresser, 1869-70, Rijksmuseum Meulag L'Aïs

You are sitting under a tree, enjoying all the comfort and quiet it is possible to find in this life, when suddenly you see a poor creature loaded with a heavy bundle coming up the narrow path opposite.
The unexpected and always striking way in which this figure appears before your eyes reminds you instantly of the sad fate of humanity - weariness. The impression is similar to that which La Fontaine expresses in his fable of the woodcutter: "Quel plaisir a-t-il eu depuis qu'il est au monde? En est-il un plus pauvre en la machine ronde?" ("Lives there between the earth and sky, so poor, so sad a wretch as I?")

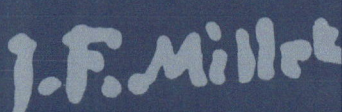

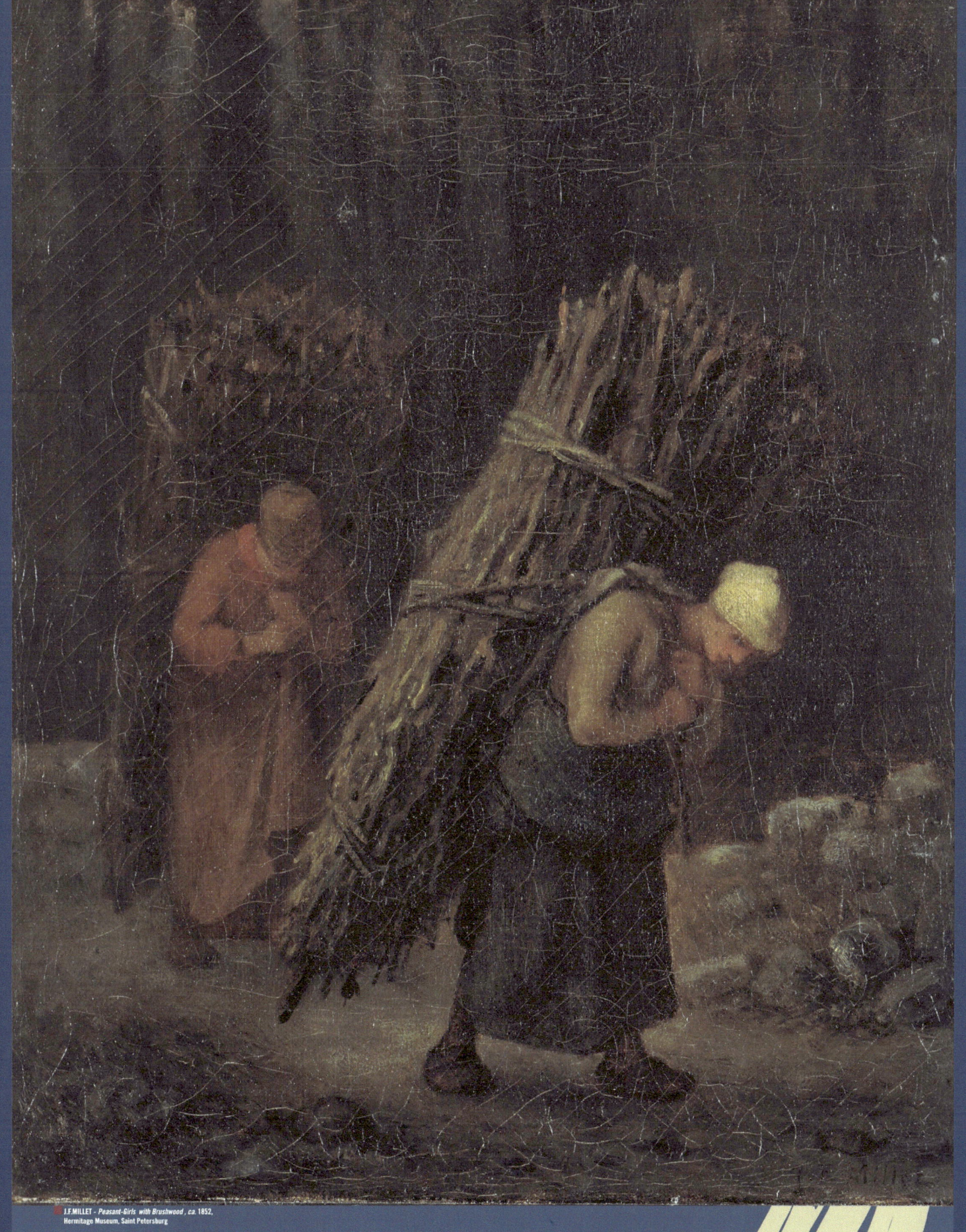

J.F. MILLET - *Peasant-Girls with Brushwood*, ca. 1852, Hermitage Museum, Saint Petersburg

J.F. Millet

DRAMA SURROUNDED BY SPLENDOR

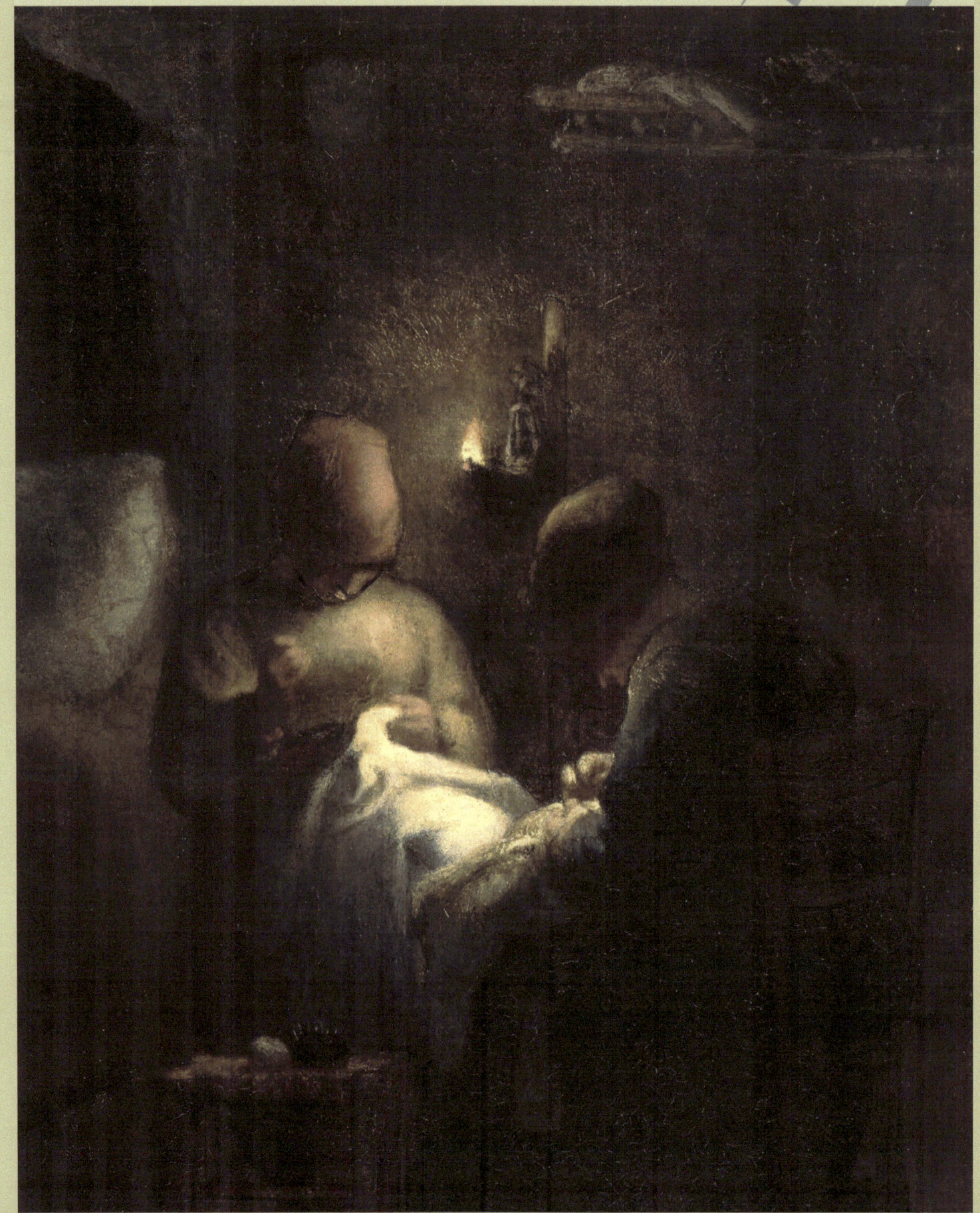

In this **second section**, we find paintings in which labor is perceived — in the words of Millet himself — as a ***drama surrounded with splendor.*** In 1855, a young American painter, Edward Wheelwright, came to Barbizon and worked with Millet for eight months. To him we are indebted for an invaluable insight into the painting of Millet, namely that the master considered artistic creation to be underpinned by **memory** — it is not sufficient simply to stare, wide-eyed; one must understand what one sees. The scenes depicted are solemn in their simplicity, and there is something of the eternal in the most commonplace instant. There is something majestic in the gestures of these humble peasant folk.

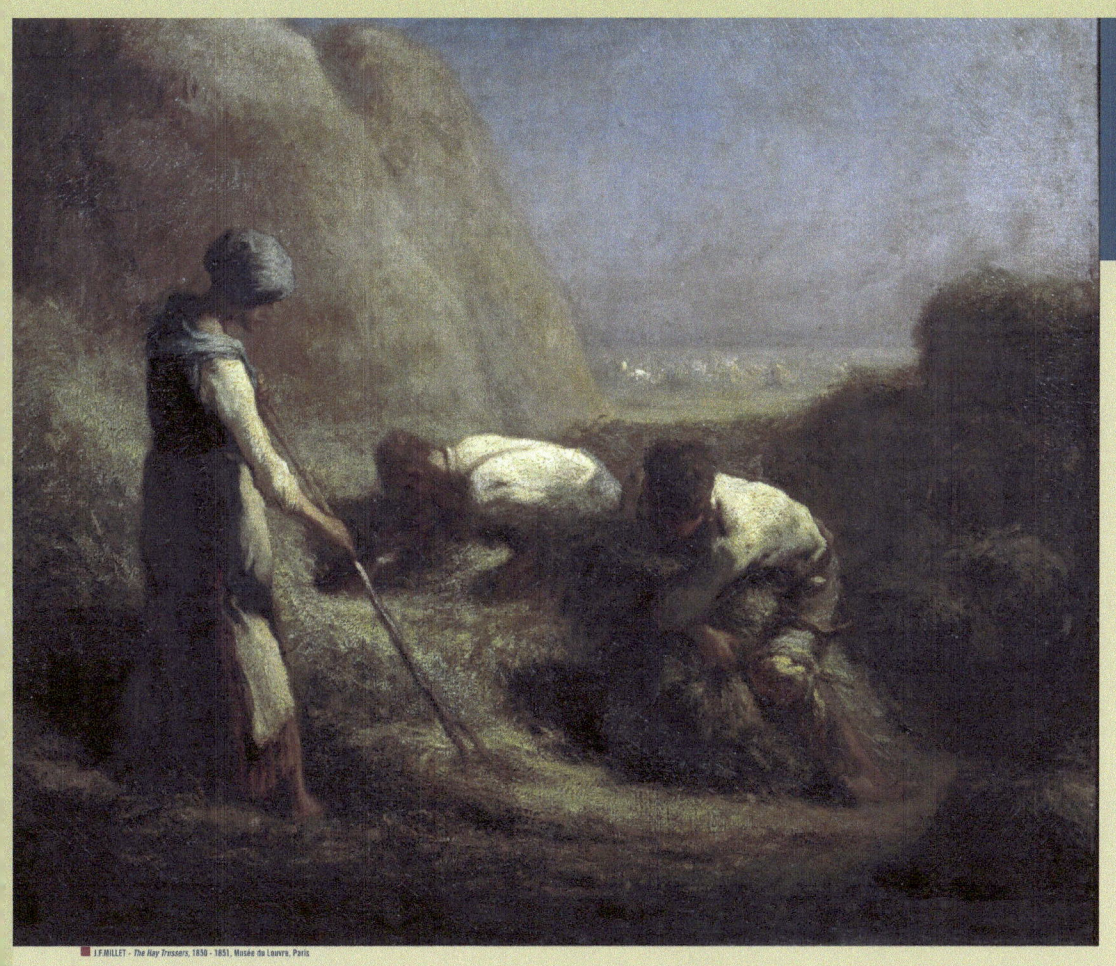

J.F.MILLET - The Hay Trussers, 1850 - 1851, Musée du Louvre, Paris

There are people who say that I see no charms in the country. I see much more than charms there: infinite splendors.
I see, as well as they do, the little flowers of which Christ said: "I say unto you, that even Solomon in all his glory was not arrayed like one of these." I see very well the aureoles of the dandelions and the sun spreading his glory in the clouds, over the distant worlds. But nonetheless I see down there in the plain the steaming horses leading the plough, and in a rocky corner a man quite worn-out, whose "ah!" has been heard since morning, and who tries to straighten himself and take breath for a moment.
The drama is surrounded with splendor. It is not my invention, and this expression, "the cry of the ground," was heard long ago. My critics are men of taste and instruction, I suppose, but I cannot put myself in their skin, and since I have never, in all my life, known anything but the fields, I try and say, as best I can, what I saw and felt when I worked there.

J.F. Millet

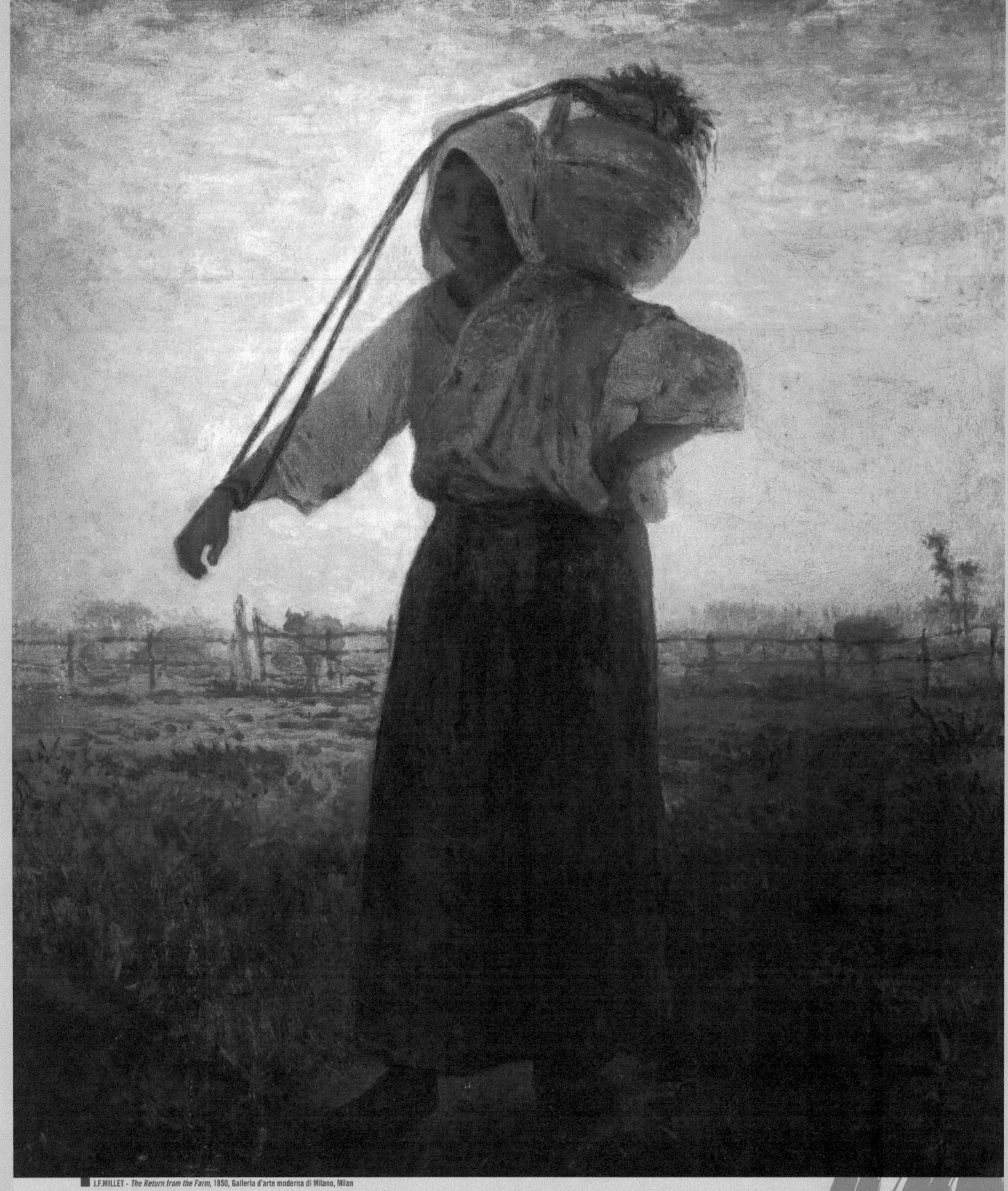

J.F.MILLET - *The Return from the Farm*, 1850, Galleria d'arte moderna di Milano, Milan

See those figures moving in the shade yonder, creeping or walking along... Surely they must be the spirits of the plain! We know they are only poor human creatures, a woman bending down under her load of hay, or dragging herself along exhausted by the weight of her bundle of wood. But far off they are superb! Look how they balance their load on their shoulders in the twilight. It is beautiful, mysterious!

J.F. Millet

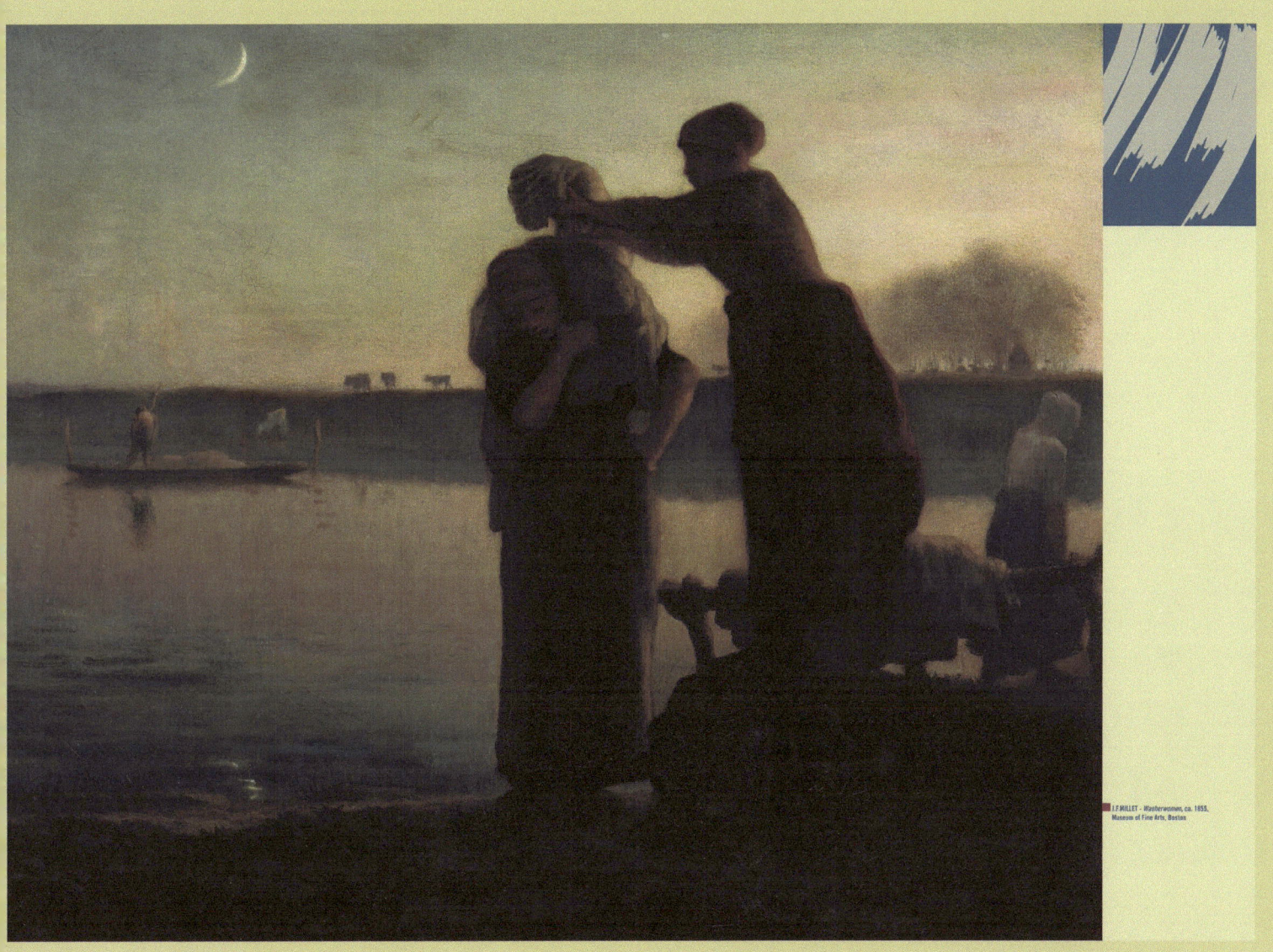

If I could only do what I like, I would paint nothing that was not the result of an impression directly received from nature, whether in landscape or in figure.   J.F. Millet

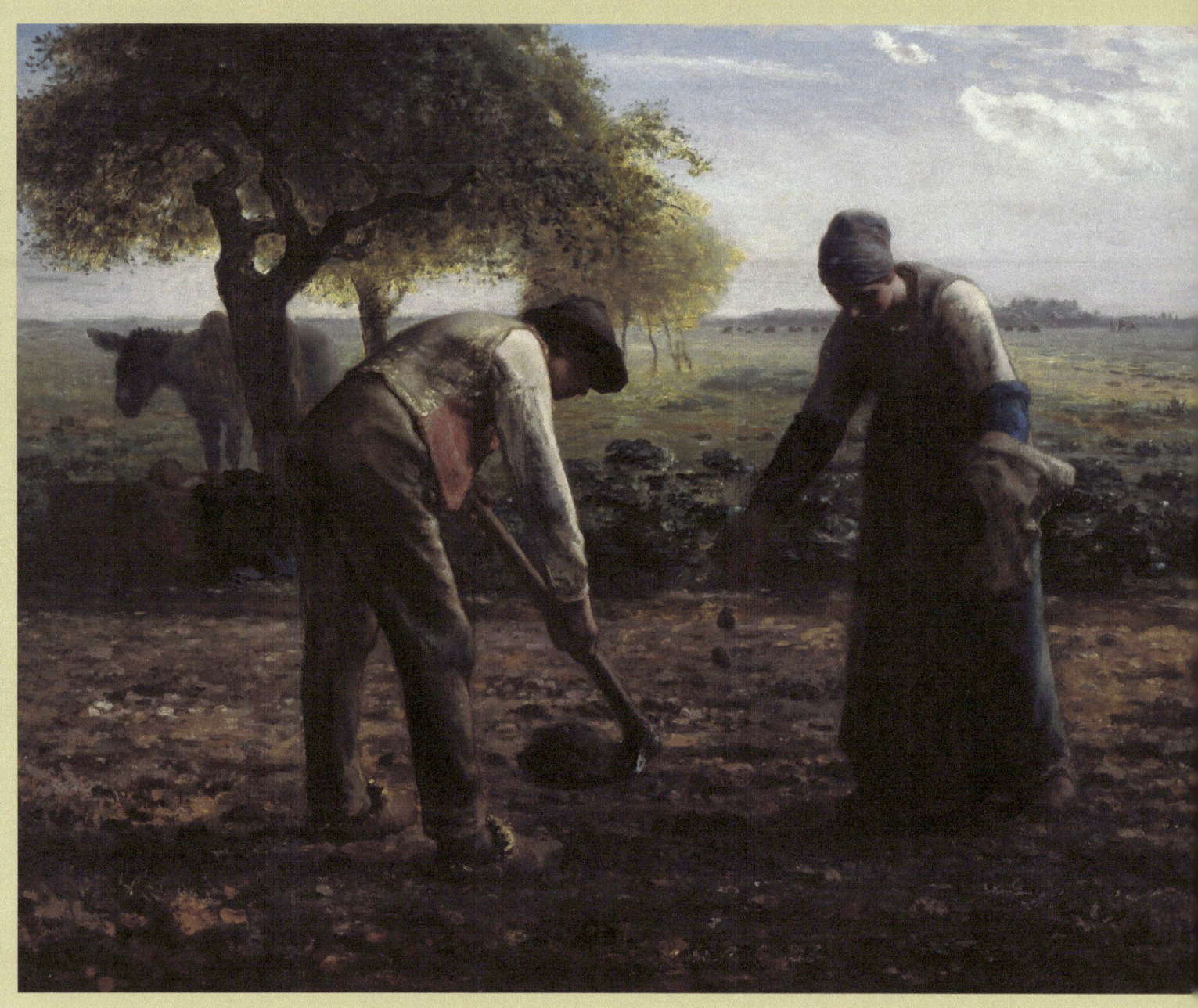

Why should the work of a potato planter or a bean planter be less interesting or less noble than any other activity? It ought to be recognized that there is not any nobility or baseness except in the manner of understanding or representing such things, and not in the things themselves. J.F. Millet

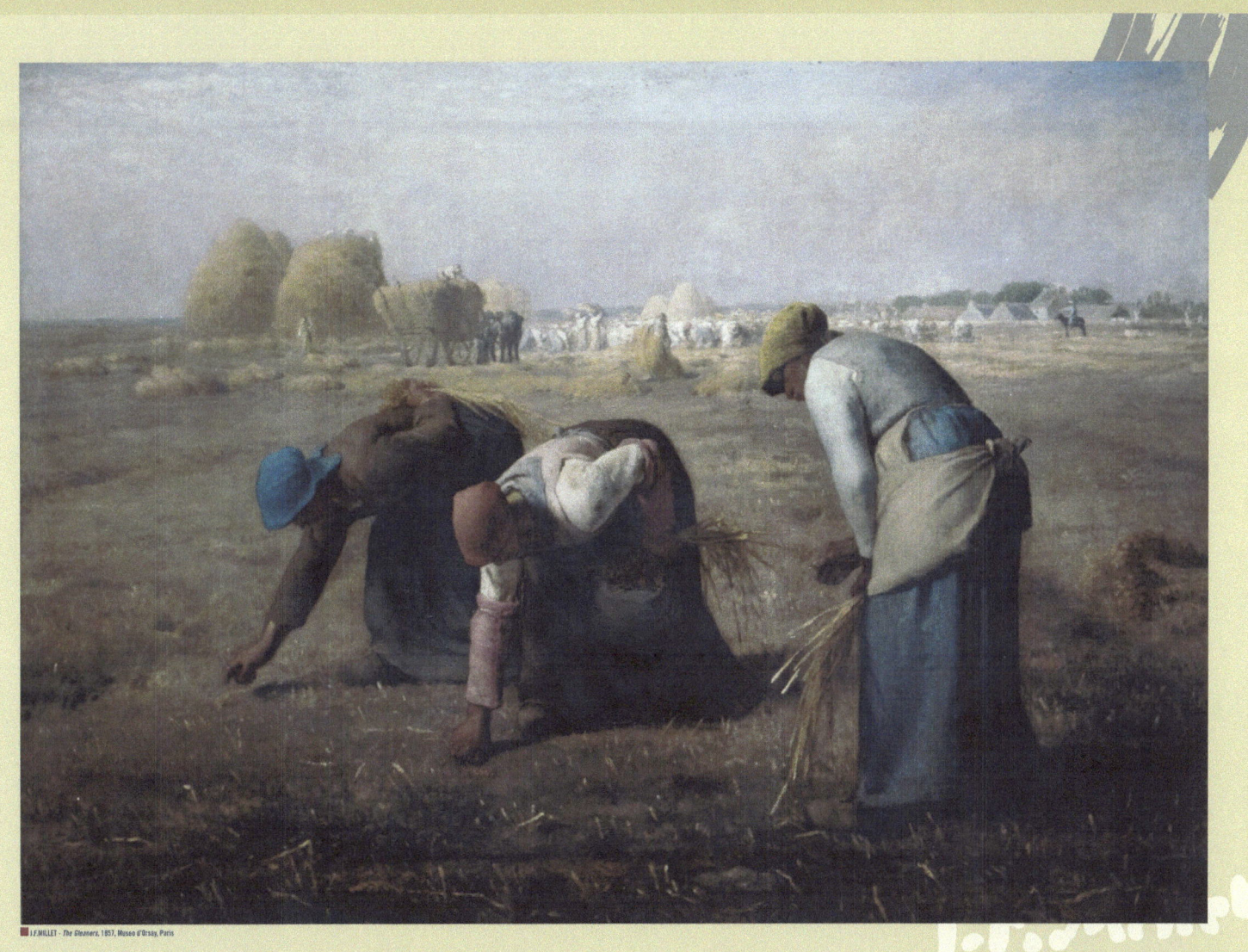

J.F.MILLET - The Gleaners, 1857, Museo d'Orsay, Paris

"Though Millet's style was considered by some to be unrefined, critics were won over by the emotional, localized color and naturalistic style with which he depicted man and his environment. Because the lives of 19th Century French peasants were inseparable from the land, so are the peasants Millet depicts. Most famously, in 1857's *The Gleaners*, farm life is accompanied by a wash of light, falling from the sky and down the arms of field hands to their harvest, confirming and easing their backbreaking labor."

- from an Artsy review

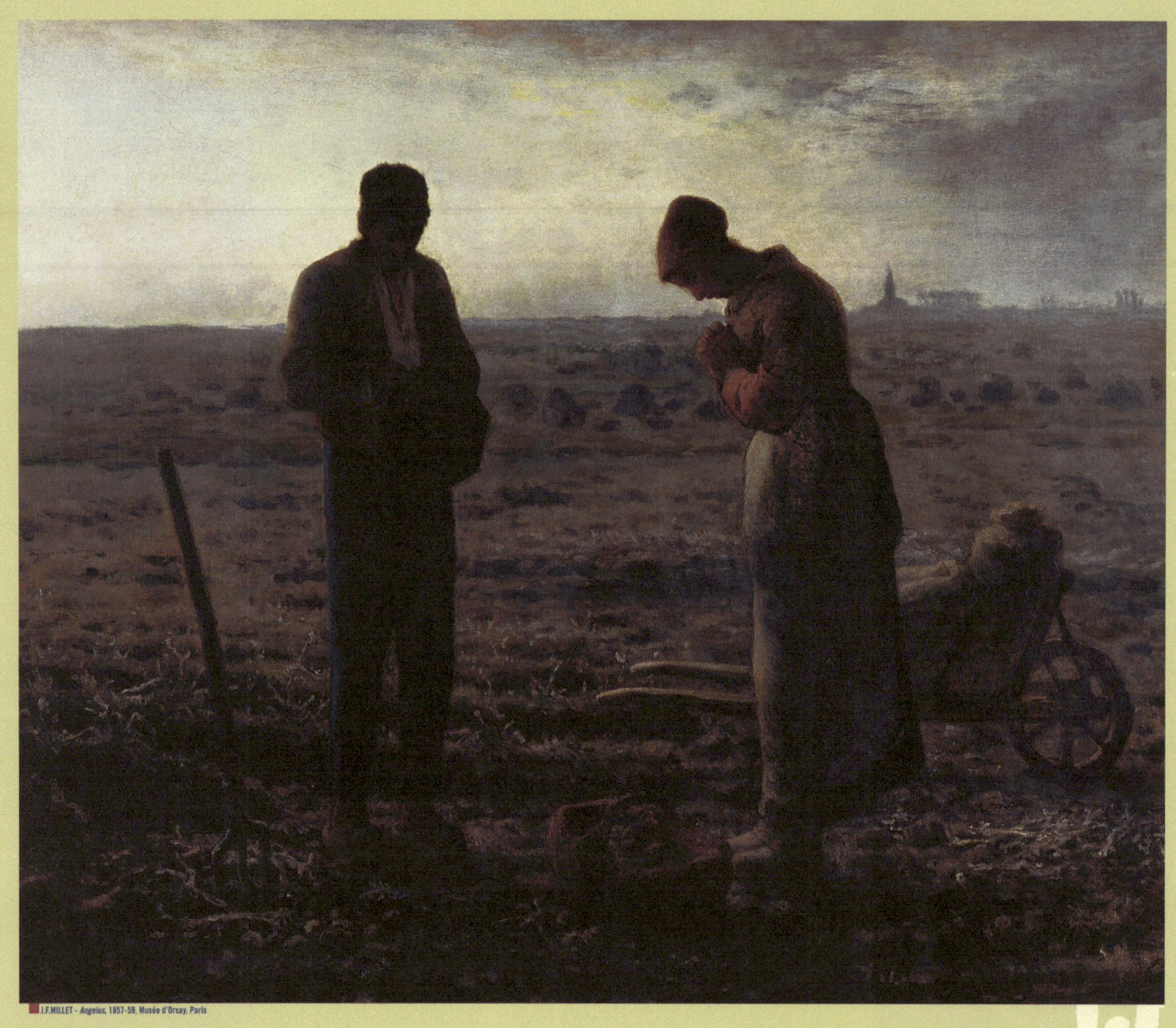

The Angelus *is a painting that I made remembering how when we used to work in the fields, at the sound of the church bells, my grandmother would always stop us in our work to say the Angelus for the poor departed, very piously and with our hats in our hands.*   J.F. Millet

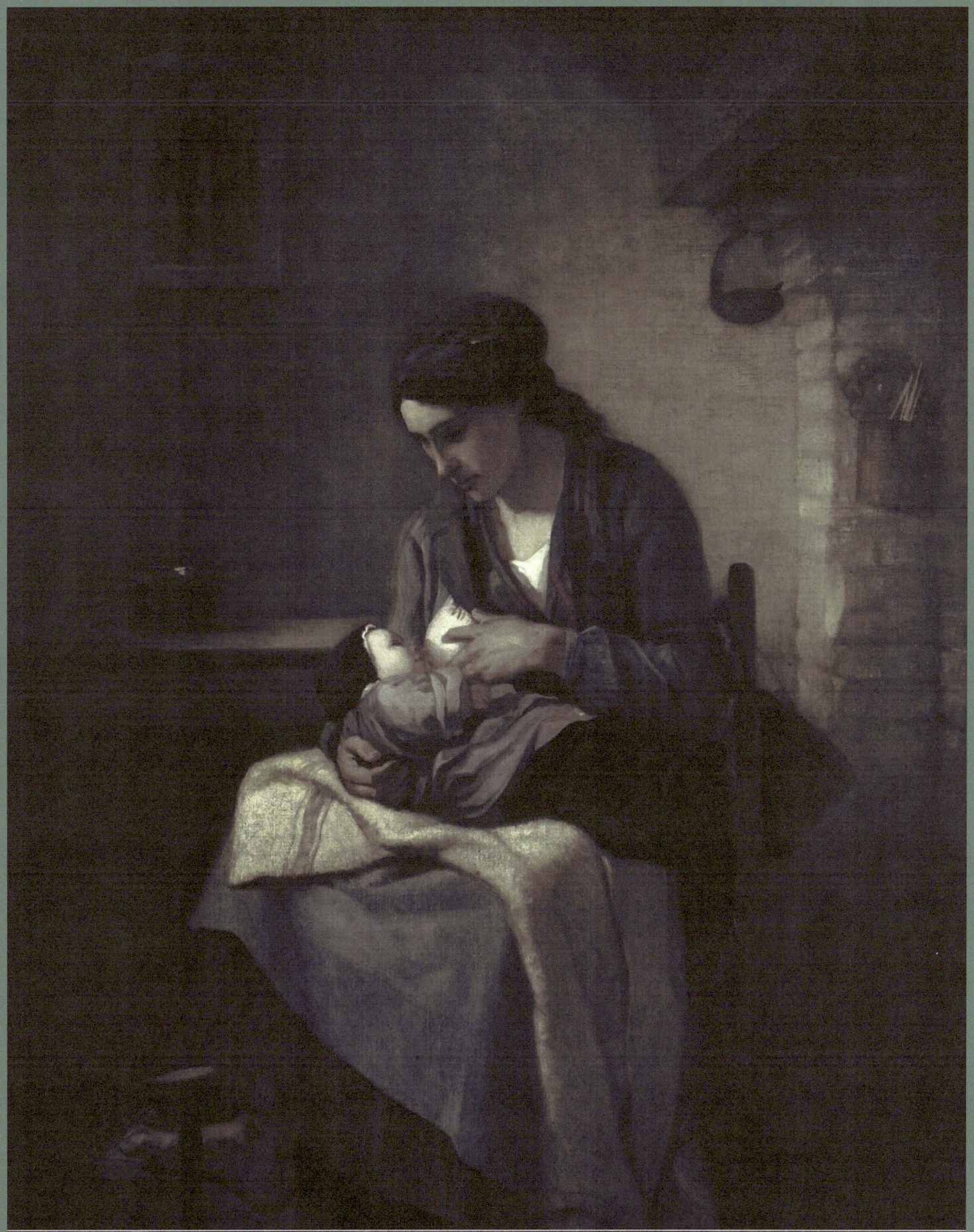

J.F. MILLET - *Peasant Woman Breastfeeding*, 1845, Musée du Louvre, Paris

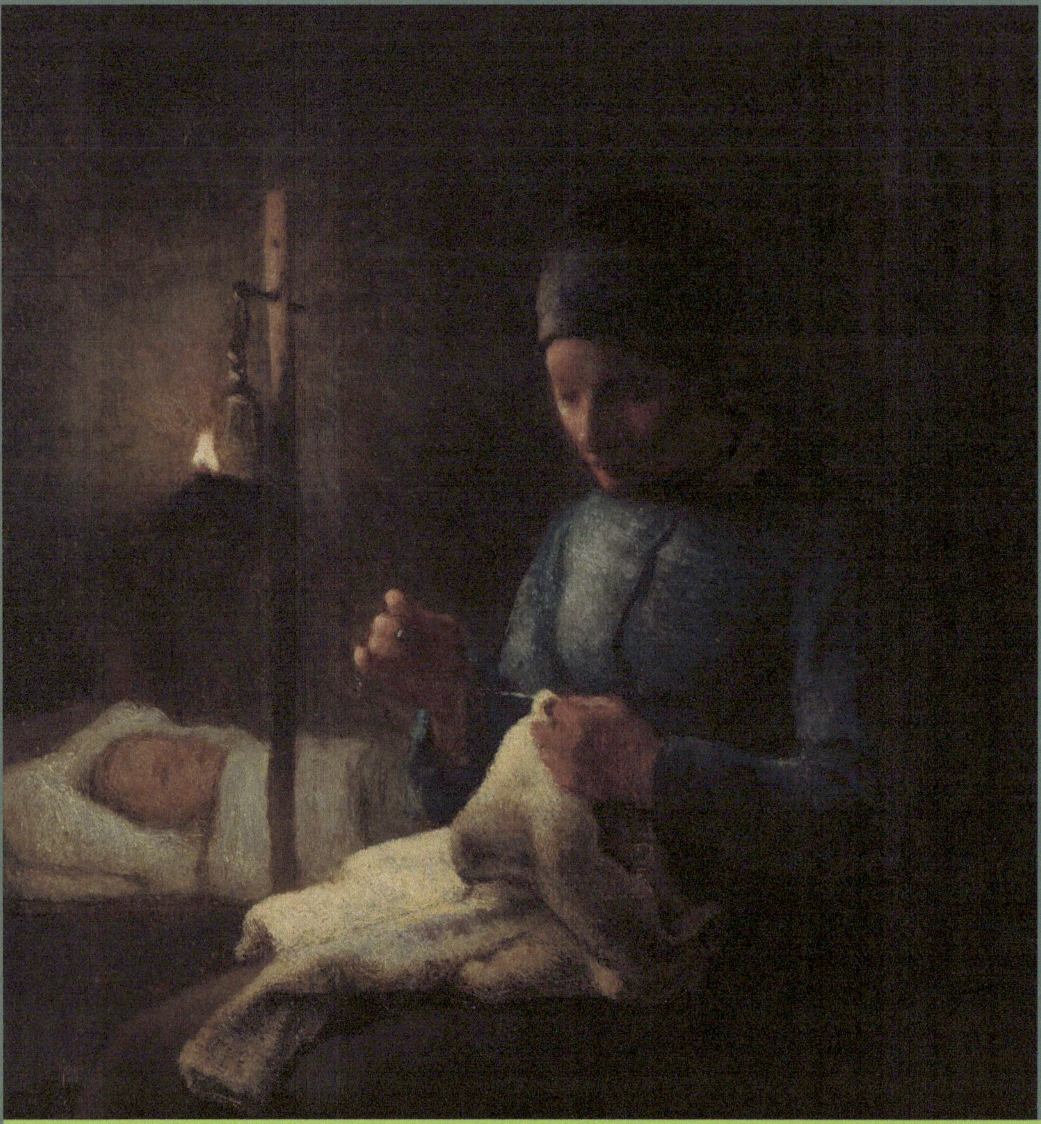

Beauty does not reside in the face; it radiates from the whole figure and appears in the appropriateness of the action to the subject. Your pretty peasant girls would be ill suited to picking up wood, gleaning in the furrows of August, or drawing water from the well. When I paint a mother, I shall try and make her beautiful, simply by the look which she bends upon her child. Beauty is expression.

J.F. MILLET - *Woman Sewing Beside her Sleeping Child*, ca. 1858-62, Museum of Fine Arts, Boston

THE LABOR OF MOTHERS

This **third section** focuses on a theme beloved of Millet the artist, who dedicated many of his paintings to women, observed while working in the fields or in the home — the paintings here acknowledge the **labor of mothers**. In these women, looking after their children and their homes, one sees the ultimate dimension of labor, which is not a commodity, but a **bountiful charity**.

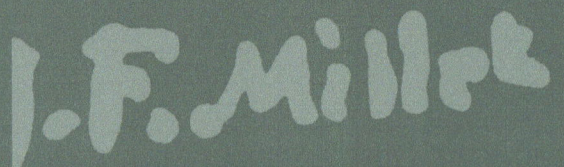

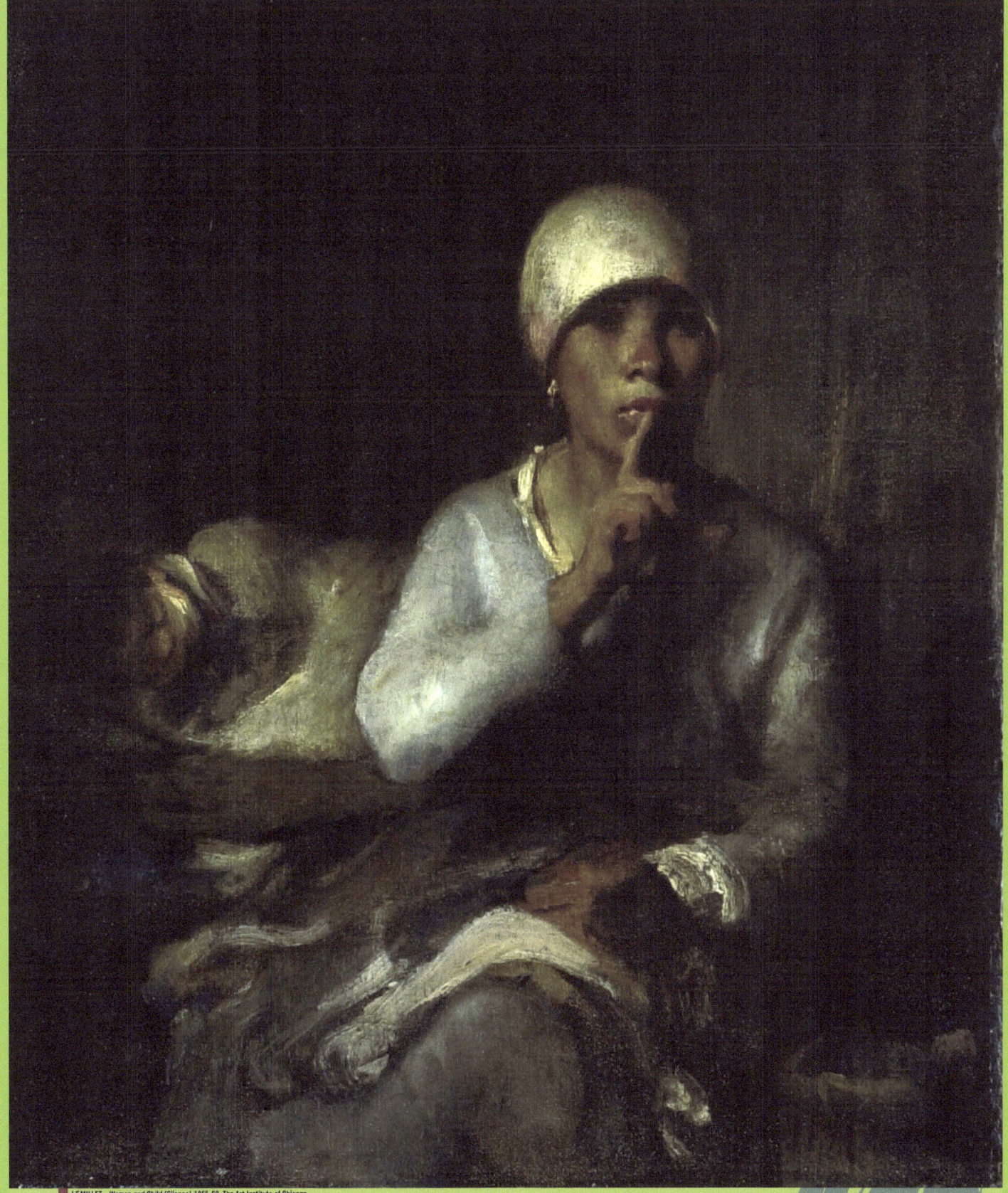

J.F.MILLET - *Woman and Child (Silence)*, 1855-60, The Art Institute of Chicago

At the bottom it always comes to this: a man must be touched himself in order to touch others, and all that is done from theory, however clever, can never attain this end, for it is impossible that it should have the breath of life. It is a sounding brass or a tinkling cymbal, to quote Saint Paul.

J.F. Millet

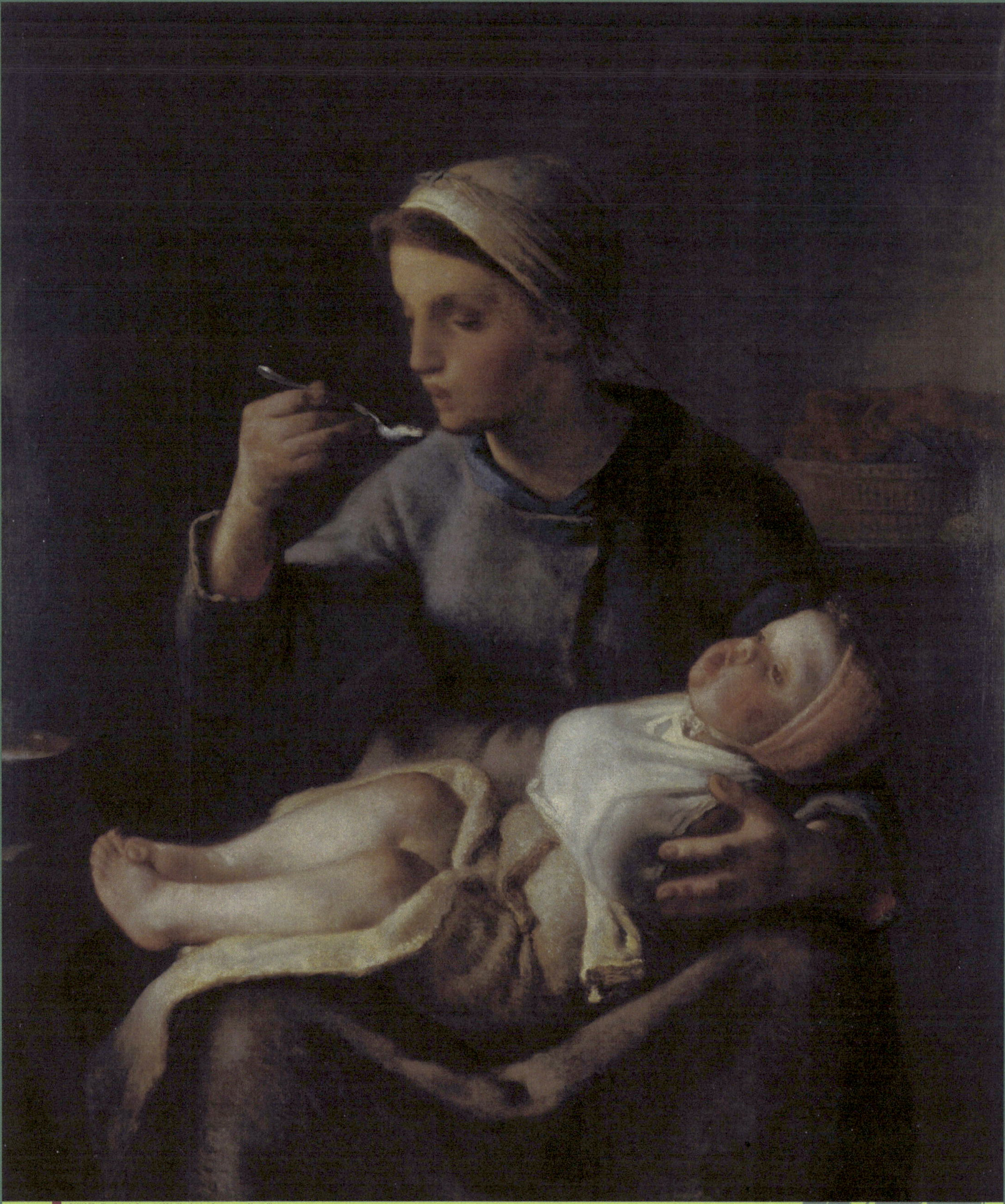

J.F.MILLET - *The Baby's Cereal*, 1861, Musée des Beaux arts, Marseille

I will do as many drawings as I can, and for as long as I can, that will capture the intimate aspect of life.

J.F. Millet

"FATHER MILLET"

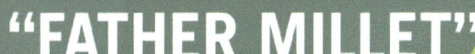
J.F. MILLET - *The Sower*, 1850, Museum of Fine Arts, Boston

Van Gogh was moved at the sight of Millet's painting: he was struck by the way the artist saw men at their labors, by the way he understood their pain, by his deeply religious perception of life. **Van Gogh** became not only a disciple, but a **son of Millet**, and reproduced many of the master's works with his own inimitable use of color. This final section looks at paintings by Millet, and the unique interpretation given to them by Van Gogh.

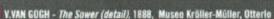
V. VAN GOGH - *The Sower (detail)*, 1888, Museo Kröller-Müller, Otterlo

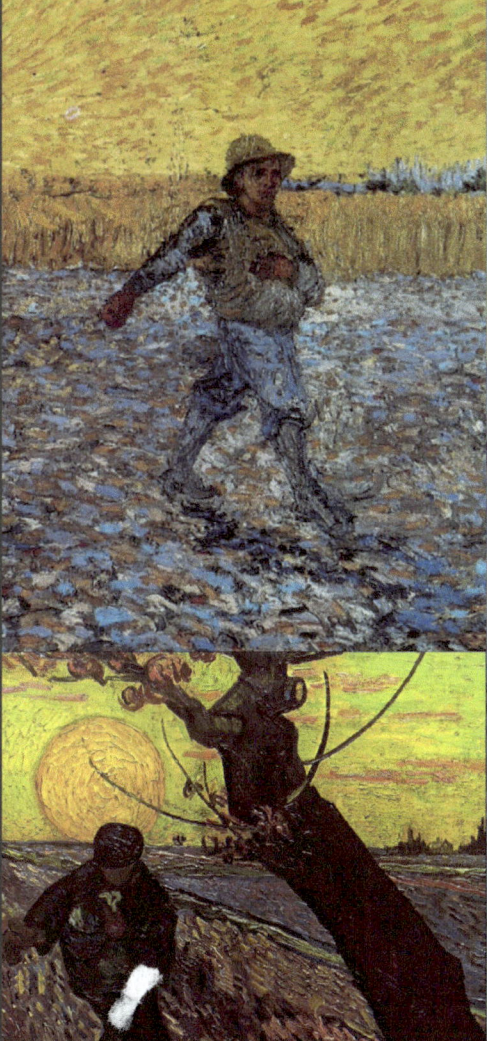

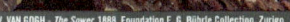
V. VAN GOGH - *The Sower*, 1888, Foundation E. G. Bührle Collection, Zurigo

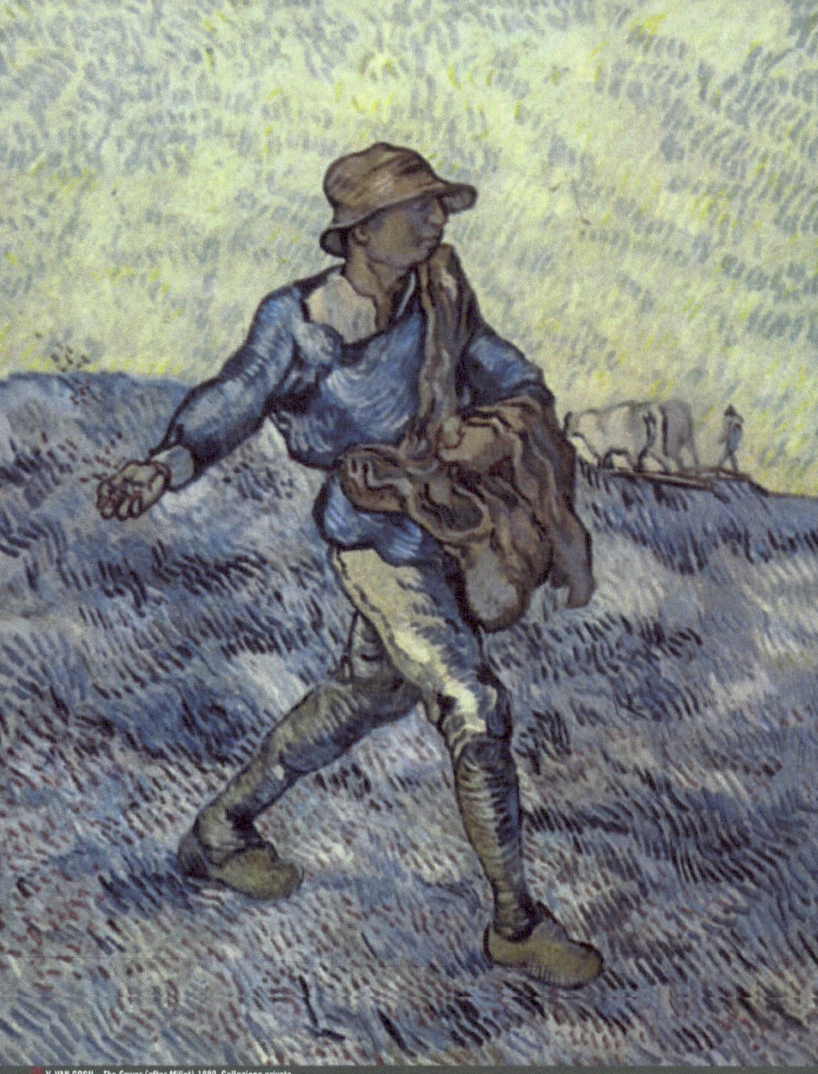
V. VAN GOGH - *The Sower (after Millet)*, 1889, Collezione privata

"Showing the figure of the peasant in action, you see that's what a figure is – I repeat – essentially modern – the heart of modern art itself. […] The figure of the peasant and the workman started more as a 'genre' – but nowadays, with Millet in the van as the eternal master, it's the very heart of modern art and will remain so."
(Vincent Van Gogh, Letter to Theo van Gogh, Nuenen, July 14, 1885, Letter No. 515)

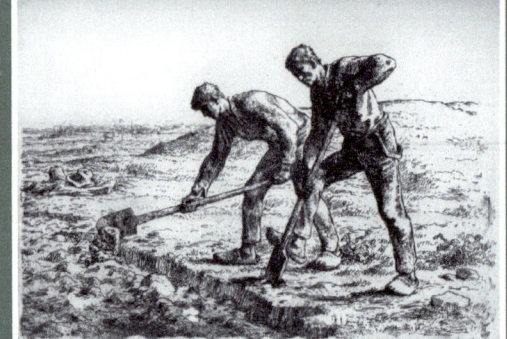
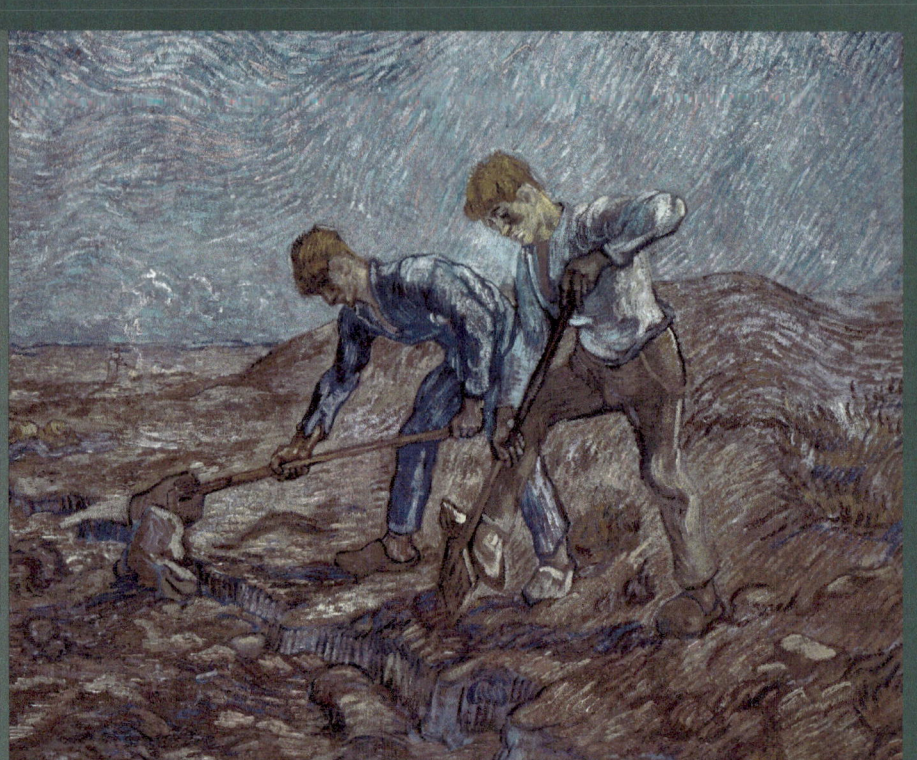

That's what Millet did – and – didn't want anything else anyway – and in my view this means that as a human being he has shown painters a way that Israëls and Mauve, say, who live quite luxuriously, do not show, and I say again – Millet is – PÈRE Millet, that is, counselor and guide in everything, for the younger painters… But I just think about what Millet said: 'I would never do away with suffering, for it is often that which makes artists express themselves most vigorously.'

(Vincent Van Gogh, Leteter to Theo van Gogh, Nuenen, April 13, 1885, Letter No. 493)

"The longer I think about it the more I see that Millet believes in a something on High. He speaks of it very differently from Pa, for instance – for he leaves it more vague, yet I see more in Millet's vagueness than in Pa. The end of things doesn't have to be an ability to explain but to base oneself on it effectively."
(Vincent Van Gogh, Letter to Theo Van Gogh, Nieuw-Amsterdam, October 31, 1883, Letter No. 401)

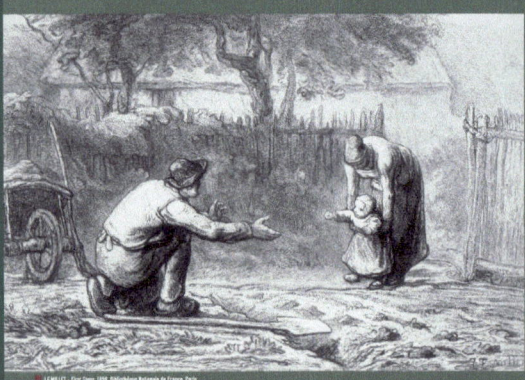
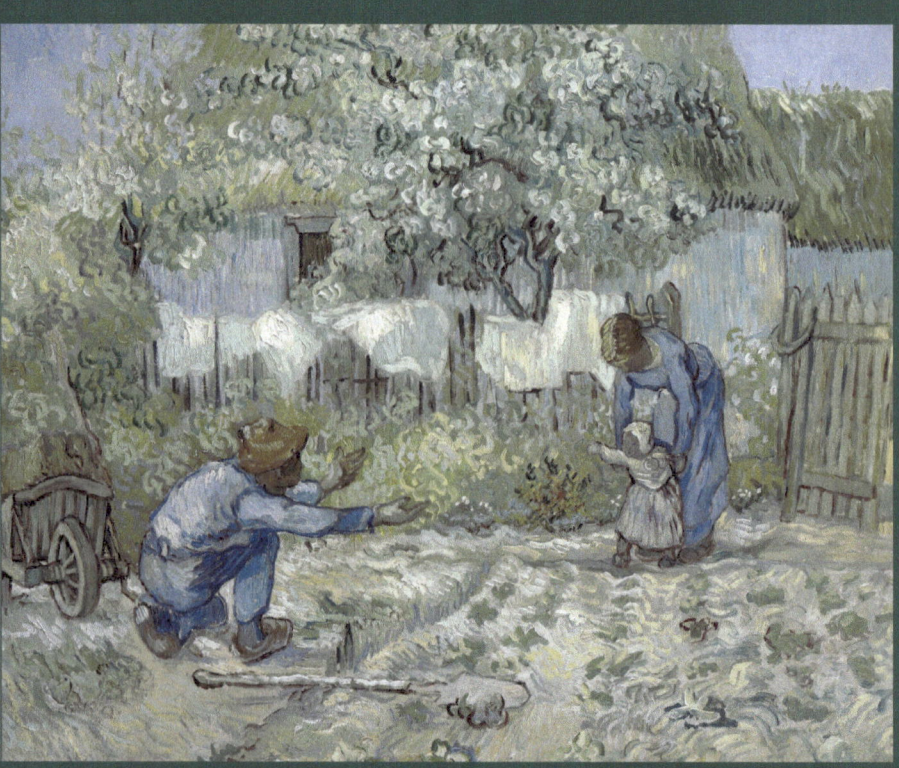

"Ah, speaking of the difference between the city and the fields, what a master Millet is. That fellow, so wise, so moved, does the countryside in such a way that even in town one continues to feel it. And then he has something unique and so good right down to his depths that it consoles one to look at his works, and one wonders if he did them this way expressly to console us."
(Vincent Van Gogh, Letter to Willemien van Gogh, Saint-Rémy-de-Provence, January 20, 1890, Letter No. 841)

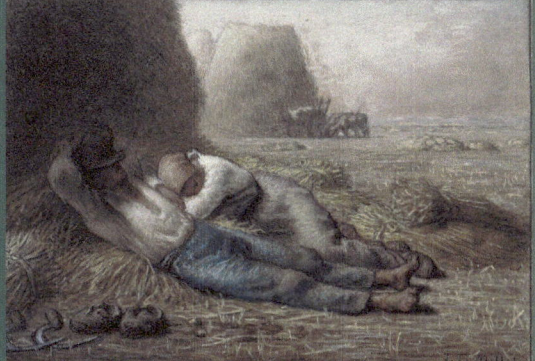
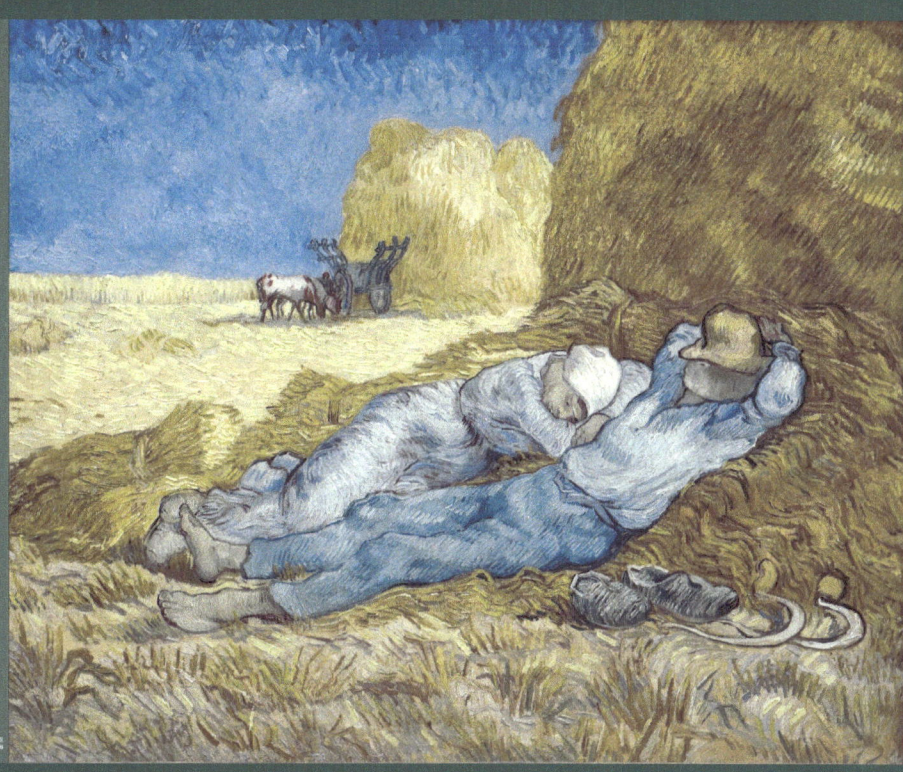

J.F. Millet

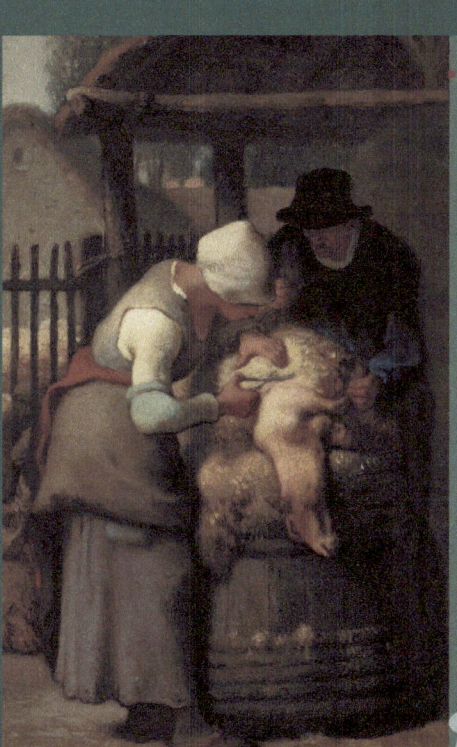

"What I'm seeking in it, and why it seems good to me to copy them, I'm going to try to tell you. We painters are always asked to compose ourselves and to be nothing but composers. Very well – but in music it isn't so – and if such a person plays some Beethoven he'll add his personal interpretation to it – in music, and then above all for singing – a composer's interpretation is something, and it isn't a hard and fast rule that only the composer plays his own compositions. Good – since I'm above all ill at present, I'm trying to do something to console myself, for my own pleasure.
I place the black-and-white by Delacroix or Millet or after them in front of me as a subject. And then I improvise color on it but, being me, not completely of course, but seeking memories of their paintings – but the memory, the vague consonance of colors that are in the same sentiment, if not right – that's my own interpretation."
(Vincent Van Gogh, Letter to Theo Van Gogh, Saint-Rémy-de-Provence, on or about Friday, 20 September 1889. Letter No. 805, http://vangoghletters.org/vg/letters/let805/letter.html)
(Vincent Van Gogh, Letter to Theo Van Gogh, Saint-Rémy-de-Provence, September 20, 1889. Letter No. 805)

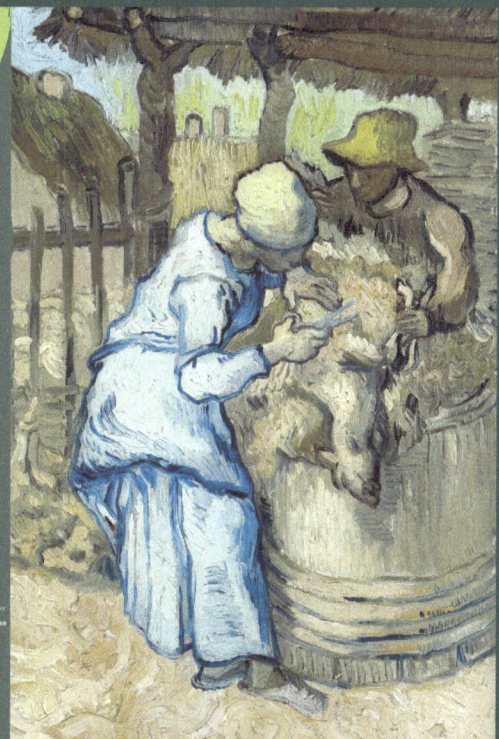

J.F. Millet

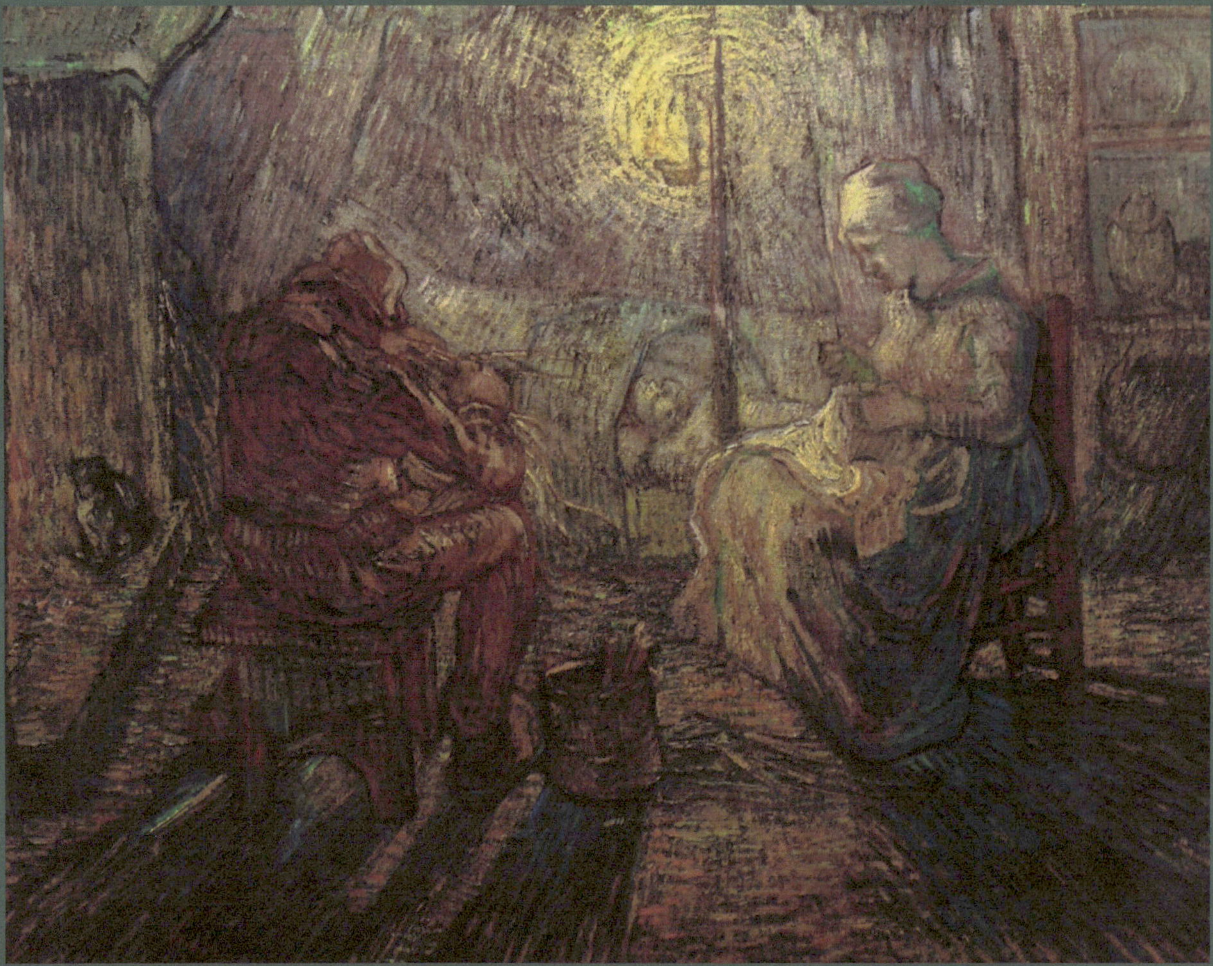

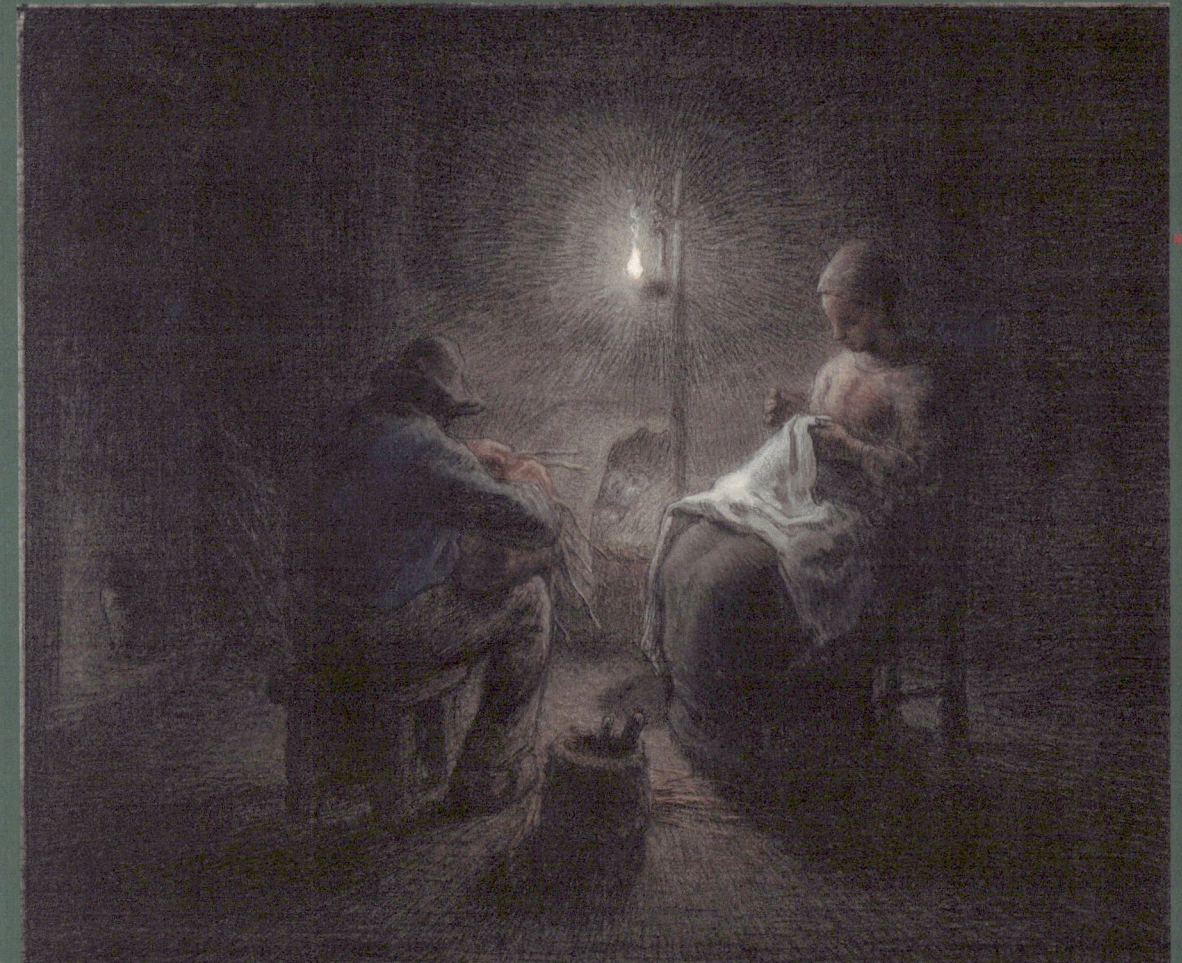

V. VAN GOGH - *Evening: the Watch (after Millet)*, 1889, Van Gogh Museum, Amsterdam

J.F. MILLET - *Winter Evening*, 1867, Museum of Fine Arts, Boston

www.ingramcontent.com/pod-product-compliance
Lightning Source LLC
Chambersburg PA
CBHW040057250526
45473CB00043B/1819